JUNIOR CYCLE
CSPE
FOURTH EDITION

CSPE IN 101 LESSONS

FOLENS
Wellbeing

[Make a Difference!]

CONOR HARRISON AND MÁIRÍN WILSON

STUDENT ACTIVITY BOOK

FOLENS

First published in 2017 by Folens Publishers
Hibernian Industrial Estate, Greenhills Road, Tallaght, Dublin 24

© Conor Harrison and Máirín Wilson, 2017

Illustrations: emcdesign except for p.61 Graham Cameron-Illustration

ISBN 978-1-78090-752-9

Photograph credits

The authors and publisher would like to thank the following for permission to use copyrighted material: Alamy; Getty Images; iStock; Photocall; Press Association; Shutterstock; UN Photo Library; Simon Kneebone.

The publisher has made every effort to contact all copyright holders but if any have been overlooked, we will be pleased to make any necessary arrangements.

Any links or references to external websites should not be construed as an endorsement by Folens of the content or views of these websites.

Contents

Acknowledgements

The authors and publisher would like to thank the following for permission to use copyrighted material: Christian Aid and CAFOD; Defence for Children International; ECO-UNESCO for Young Environmentalist Awards; Enable Ireland; Fairtrade; An Garda Síochána; The Garda Reserve; Irish Traveller's Movement; ISTE® (International Society for Technology in Education); Limerick City and County Council; Oxfam; Pavee Point; UNHCR; UNICEF; UNDP; United Nations; WaterAid. Evoke; Irish Daily Star; Irish Farmers Journal; The Irish Times; The Irish Independent Group; Irish Examiner; Trinity Mirror; News Group Newspapers Limited; Journal Media. *Being LGBT in Schools* was published by GLEN, the LGBTI equality network, with the support of the Department of Education and Skills. 'The Newcomer' from *Gargling with Jelly* by Brian Patten. Published by Puffin, 1986. Copyright © Brian Patten. Reproduced by permission of the author c/o Rogers, Coleridge & White Ltd., 20 Powis Mews, London W11 1JN.

Participating in society

Welcome to CSPE

CSPE is a new course of study for you over the next three years. It is important that you know what these letters stand for, so fill in the blanks below.
C _____, S _____, and P _____ E _____.

This is a course about being a citizen, both locally and globally. CSPE is about human rights and living in a responsible way in today's world.

CSPE is part of a new area of learning called Wellbeing along with Social, Personal and Health Education (SPHE), PE and Guidance. Together these subjects join up to cover some key areas that help you to develop as a healthy, informed, caring and responsible person. CSPE helps you to think and learn about yourself as a citizen.

The course is built on three strands and eight themes, or ideas, listed below. Match the themes in blue with the correct strand in orange.

Rights and responsibilities · Global citizenship · Exploring democracy

Sustainability (development that will last into the future) · The meaning of democracy · Human rights instruments (documents) · Effective global change · The law and the citizen · Local and global development · Human dignity, the basis for human rights · The role of the media in a democracy

Start gathering ideas, work, pictures, articles and information to capture your learning in CSPE – like you are doing a project. It is also a really good idea to note your own thoughts and learning every so often – like in a diary or a blog.

My wellbeing

FOLENS
Wellbeing

My name: _____

5 Things I need to be physically well.
_____
_____
_____
_____
_____
_____

5 Things I need to be mentally well.
_____
_____
_____
_____
_____
_____

5 Things I need to be well socially.
_____
_____
_____
_____
_____
_____

5 Things I need to be a 'well' citizen.
_____
_____
_____
_____
_____
_____

The citizenship rap

Add in your own verse to this rap on the blank lines below, then get together in a group to say/perform the rap aloud.

Citizen, citizen – active citizen.

Don't throw litter on the ground

Put it in the bins that are all around.

The world is precious, guard it well

It's under threat, I've heard tell

Citizen, citizen – active citizen.

When you are 18 you must go

To cast your vote, to show you know

That you can choose who you want in

To elect the one you want to win.

Citizen, citizen – active citizen.

Obey the law, you know it's right

Don't vandalise, rob things or fight

Pay your taxes, careful when you drive,

Know the rules, arrive alive.

Citizen, citizen – active citizen.

Care for the old, the homeless, the poor.

Open your heart, be there for sure.

Look out for your neighbours, it's easy to do

Be an active citizen. It starts with you!

Citizen, citizen – active citizen.

_____

_____

_____

Citizen, citizen – active citizen.

Some people here are carrying signs about active citizens. Fill in the signs of the other people that are blank. Each sign should tell something about being an active citizen.

Star citizens

Put the names of some local star citizens and some national ones in the stars below.

Choose any **one** of the star citizens above and explain what that person has done to make a difference in your community or in Ireland.

_____
_____
_____
_____
_____
_____
_____
_____

Portfolio cover

Design the cover for your First Year CSPE Portfolio.

Extra, extra! Read all about it!

News headlines tell us about important events.

1. Write down **three** real headlines about things happening in the world today.
    Find one local, one national and one global headline.

2. Choose **one** of the headlines and, in your copy, explain the story behind it with at least
    three pieces of information.

LOCAL NEWS HEADLINE

NATIONAL NEWS HEADLINE

GLOBAL NEWS HEADLINE

The media and me

Examine this illustration and jot down the many different types of media that you can spot in the space provided.

_____

_____

_____

_____

_____

_____

What challenges and what opportunities do you think exist for us as a society when it comes to our use of today's media?

Challenges   **Opportunities**

_____   _____

_____   _____

_____   _____

_____   _____

_____   _____

 # Human dignity: the basis for human rights

Overview of human dignity: the basis for human rights

Respecting human dignity is the basis of human rights. Once you understand what human dignity is then you will see that having human rights makes sense. Human dignity is about the basic needs that all people have because they are all born with the dignity of human beings. These needs include clean air and water, proper food and shelter, an education, protection from harm, security, respect and love.

When studying human dignity, you will look at the many ways people's human dignity is respected and sometimes how it is denied. Human rights is one way of trying to ensure that all people are treated with dignity and worth.

On a personal level, we are called to respect the dignity of all human beings and not to discriminate against people because of where they live, how they look, because of their nationality or colour, because of their poverty or wealth, their disabilities or religious beliefs.

Society takes its responsibility seriously and tries to ensure that nothing happens that reduces the human dignity of any person. Governments ensure that laws passed always respect people's dignity.

Sadly, not everybody's human dignity is respected. People are starving and homeless, people are bullied and jeered at, and people live in poverty. In some parts of the world, people's human dignity is denied to them for different reasons: because of natural disasters such as famine or drought, at times of war, where there is a bad leader or because they are living in a country that is still developing.

Human rights for a new planet

A new planet has been discovered and people are going to move there to live. Your job is to write a **Declaration of Human Rights** for the people who will live there. This declaration can have 10 rights in it.

1. List the 10 rights you would have in the chart below.

2. Match the rights you have chosen to the UDHR.

Rights for the new planet	UDHR

3. Explain the purpose of any **two** rights you have chosen for your new planet.

_____

_____

_____

_____

_____

_____

I was hungry …

1. Match the needs on the left with the words on the right.

air	shelter
water	wear
a home	breathe
clothes	love
food	eat
friends	drink

2. Read the poem below and answer the questions that follow.

I WAS HUNGRY

And you fed your animals with my food.

I WAS HUNGRY

And your multinationals planted your winter tomatoes on our best land.

I WAS HUNGRY

And you wouldn't give up your steak from South America.

I WAS HUNGRY

And they grew coffee for you where corn might grow for my daily meal.

I WAS HUNGRY

But you turned our sugar cane and manioc* into fuel for your cars.

I WAS HUNGRY

But the waste from your factories is poisoning the fishing grounds of the Earth.

I WAS HUNGRY

But with your money you bought up all my food.

I WAS HUNGRY

While my land grows exotic food for your table.

*Manioc is a root vegetable that can be turned into flour.

Source: *We Ask Why They Are Hungry, Christian Aid and CAFOD*

(a) Name and explain how the needs of any **two** groups from this poem were placed before the needs of this hungry person.

_____

_____

_____

_____

(b) Suggest **one** action that the Irish government could take to try to end world hunger.

_____

_____

_____

_____

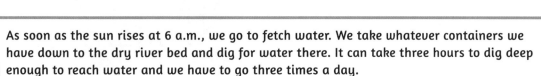

Water is my life – nine hours

In Burkina Faso, West Africa, Segueda Zouga has no choice but to spend nine hours a day collecting dirty water from a hole. Not only is it unsafe to drink, but the long daily trek means Segueda has no time left to earn a living.

> As soon as the sun rises at 6 a.m., we go to fetch water. We take whatever containers we have down to the dry river bed and dig for water there. It can take three hours to dig deep enough to reach water and we have to go three times a day.
>
> I have had six children but only two of them have survived. My only choice is to give them water that is not safe to drink, or no water at all. I worry about the water I give them constantly. We get ill often. My children and I get fevers, stomach cramps and diarrhoea. Many people in the village die.
>
> Water is the biggest problem in my life and in the lives of the other families in this village. All day I think about nothing else. At night, I go to sleep worrying about fetching water and about what will happen if there is no water for us to fetch tomorrow. All of us go, old women, young women, pregnant women – even the children. We all have to do our bit. I know the children should go to school, but what choice do we have? What use is an education if I can't give my children enough water to drink?

Water is the community's biggest problem, but now WaterAid has plans to work with them and help them build a safe water supply. Once it is complete, life will be different here.

People who have access to clean water and sanitation have better health and more time to improve their children's education, food and family income; they also spend less on medicine.

> If I didn't have to spend nine hours a day fetching water, I could do so much more. Sometimes I try to spin the cotton we grow to weave cloth and make clothes, with maybe some left over to sell, but I hardly even have time to do this. If we had water, my children could go to school and I would be able to spend time growing more food and cleaning the compound.

Source: *WaterAid/Mike Wade*

1. Draw **four** pictures/cartoons/images in the boxes provided that illustrate four different aspects of Segueda Zouga's life.

2. What difference would it make to Segueda Zouga's life if she had water easily available to her?

_____

_____

_____

_____

Humanitarian crisis

A hurricane has created a natural disaster in a country far away. This has caused flooding and destruction. Millions of people have been left without their basic needs, such as clean water, shelter and medicine. Many thousands of people have died. This is a humanitarian crisis. You and your friends want to do something to help.

1. Name **one** organisation that you could contact that would help at a time like this. Give **two** reasons why you would choose that particular organisation.

   Organisation:

   _____

   Reasons:

   _____

   _____

   _____

   _____

   _____

   _____

   _____

2. Write a short article that you could send to your local newspaper trying to get more support for this cause.

   _____

   _____

   _____

   _____

   _____

   _____

   _____

3. Describe **two** actions that a community could do to help at a time like this.

   _____

   _____

   _____

   _____

   _____

   _____

   _____

Disabled driver's parking space

FOLENS
Wellbeing

1. Some parking spaces have special symbols put on them to remind people that they are only for the use of people with disabilities. Do you think that this is right? Explain your answer.

_____

_____

_____

_____

_____

2. Design your own parking space reminder-card that you could put on the windscreen of a car that has been wrongly parked in a space for a person with disabilities in your school car park.

The language of disability

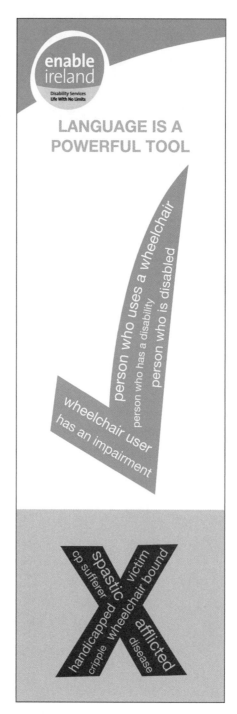

Take a close look at this bookmark produced by Enable Ireland and answer the questions below.

1. What 'powerful tool' is this bookmark about?

2. According to the bookmark, 'wheelchair bound' is not the right phrase to use. What is?

3. Give **two** examples of correct words to use when talking about people with disabilities.

4. The Special Olympics and the Paralympics celebrate people with disabilities. Why is it important to have these kinds of events?

5. Describe **two** actions that your class could take to raise awareness about the human dignity and the rights of people with disabilities.

Irish sign language

Sign language allows deaf people to talk and communicate with each other.
From the diagrams below, learn to sign your name.

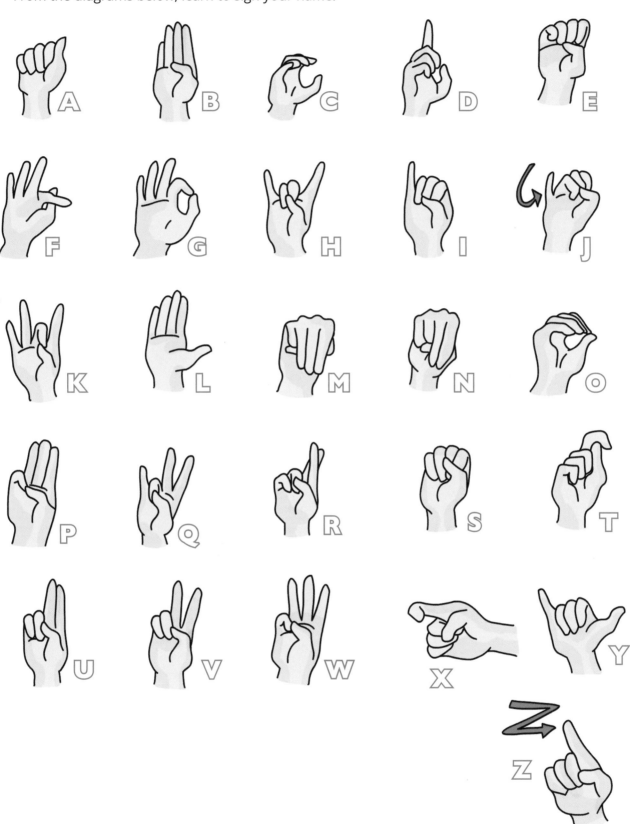

Human rights rhymes

Read the verses below as if they were nursery rhymes.

1. Justice and freedom (Jack and Jill)

Justice and freedom went up a hill

To fetch a Human Rights Charter

Justice fell down and broke his crown

And freedom came tumbling after.

2. Eleanor (Mary, Mary quite contrary)

Eleanor, Eleanor, quite a lady

How much the world owes to you

With a human rights vision and a worldwide mission

And a dream that is lasting and true.

3. Discrimination (Baa baa black sheep)

Baa baa discrimination

Where are you today?

Yes, sir, yes, sir

You're here in every way.

One, you're the homeless

Two, the refugee alone

Three, you're the little child in a war zone.

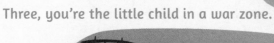

4. Fear (Sing a song of sixpence)

Sing a song of freedom

A pocket full of fear

Five million soldiers came

Destroyed our life here

And when the fear was broken

No one could ever rise

Isn't that an awful thing

To put before our eyes?

5. Human rights (Humpty Dumpty)

Human rights are still not for all

Human rights could have a big fall

All the world's leaders and all the world's plans

Must try to turn people into human rights fans!

6. On the street (There was an old woman who lived in a shoe)

There was a young woman who lived on the street

She had so many problems and nothing to eat

She begged and she stole and she had no bed

And nobody cared or would know she was dead.

7. The bully (Hickory, dickory dock)

Hickory, dickory dock

The bullying has to stop

No one should cause hurt

'Cos we all have a worth

Hickory, dickory dock.

8. War (One-two-buckle-my-shoe)

One, two, it's up to you

Three, four, to stop the war

Five, six, to find the fix

Seven, eight, it's not too late

Nine, ten, never again!

9. Homeless (Clap hands)

Clap hands 'til you find a home

With holes in your pocket

and you all alone ...

1. Think of another rhyme and rewrite it to raise awareness of human rights. Or rewrite one of the rhymes above.

2. Copy out these rhymes and make a display of them, perhaps for International Human Rights Day on 10 December.

Picture this!

A refugee camp with lots of tents and ragged children and adults queueing for food.

Do you really need a picture?

1. What is the message in this picture?

_____

_____

_____

_____

_____

_____

2. Is this picture a good way to get across a message? Explain your answer.

_____

_____

_____

_____

_____

_____

Human rights

Overview of human rights

This chapter is about human rights. What are human rights? People often describe them by listing the ones that they know. Sometimes, people confuse human rights with personal wants or needs. The word 'rights' and the phrase 'I have a right to …' are often used by people to make a point, but they are not used properly.

A right is a freedom of some kind; it is something to which you are entitled because you are human. Every human being is entitled to each and every one of them. Human rights have been written down in a number of important documents that we call human rights instruments, such as the Universal Declaration of Human Rights (UDHR) and the European Convention on Human Rights (ECHR).

Human rights mean such things as the right to freedom, the right to a name and nationality, the right to an opinion, the right to practise your religion and the right to a fair trial.

Children's rights are also named in a separate instrument, called the UN Convention on the Rights of the Child (UNCRC), which sets out these rights. Many countries have signed up to all of these instruments. This means that they must take human rights and children's rights into account when they are passing laws.

In some countries around the world, people's human rights are denied, and human rights abuses can be found in most societies. While some countries deny freedom to people, in others the human rights of some groups are not met. As a result, human rights organisations and activists campaign to help groups whose rights are being denied. For example, they fight for the human rights of the elderly, for people with disabilities, for Travellers, for LGBT people, and for asylum seekers and refugees.

Protecting human rights and fighting for them is the responsibility of everyone; this side of human rights is explored in Chapter 4.

The rights pictures

From any of the human rights instruments pick out any **three** rights and draw a picture to explain each of the rights you have chosen. It might be a good idea to share out the rights in the class, then take photos of what the class has come up with and make a wall display/PowerPoint presentation.

The right to_____

The right to_____

The right to_____

Stereo-drawing

Picture A

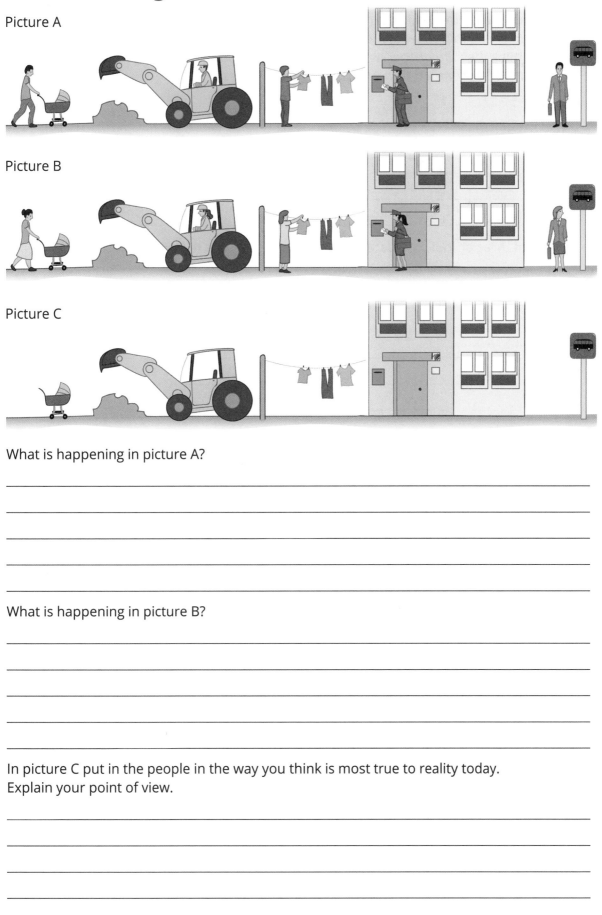

Picture B

Picture C

What is happening in picture A?

_____

_____

_____

_____

_____

What is happening in picture B?

_____

_____

_____

_____

_____

In picture C put in the people in the way you think is most true to reality today.
Explain your point of view.

_____

_____

_____

_____

_____

Men and women

Look at the words below. If you think they are associated with men put an M beside them, if you think they are associated with women put a W beside them. And if you think they are neither associated with men or women then put an E beside them for 'either men or women'.

FOLENS
Wellbeing

Strong		Determined		Beautiful		Computer whizz	
Pretty		Shy		Eejit		Kind	
Gentle		Cold		Bread-winner		Frightened	
Confident		Hunk		Clever		Hot	
Caring		Emotional		Joker		Dominant	

In groups of three or four, compare your lists. What does this tell you about stereotyping?

_____

_____

_____

_____

_____

_____

Recent research shows that girls are getting higher points than boys in the Leaving Certificate, why do you think that might be? Are you stereotyping when you answer this?

_____

_____

_____

_____

Lowtown

Imagine a town called Lowtown, it was built for wheelchair users only. Everything is geared specially for them. Ceilings are low, doorways are all wide, houses are on one level.

Imagine then that some able-bodied people come to live in Lowtown. They bump their heads on doors and have to crouch down in rooms, shops, schools and other buildings. They are disabled by their height.

Special helmets are designed for these disabled people. Special supports are made to help keep their backs bent as a protection for them. They find it difficult to get to work because they look out of place with their big helmets and special back supports.

However, twice a year the town holds a fundraiser for these people. They are even talking about building special homes and redesigning cars and buses to allow them to travel with some comfort.

1.   Imagine that you were living in Lowtown. How would you feel about living in such a world?

_____

_____

_____

_____

2.   What does this story tell us about disability?

_____

_____

_____

_____

_____

3.   Today, how are the needs of people with disabilities catered for in your community?

_____

_____

_____

_____

_____

The migrant crisis

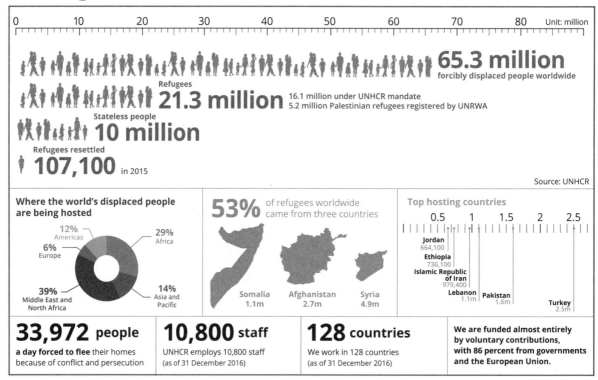

Study the infographic above and answer the following questions.

1. According to the UN High Commission for Refugees how many refugees are there in the world at the moment?

   _____

   _____

2. How many people have been displaced from their homes?

   _____

   _____

3. Name **three** countries that account for 53 per cent of the world's refugees:

   _____

   _____

   _____

4. Name **two** reasons why people become displaced within their own countries or refugees abroad.

5. A local person is trying to fill a truck with supplies to send to a refugee camp in Europe. Your **class** want to support this effort by collecting food and other goods. Name **three** key people or groups of people you would have to communicate with to make this collection happen. Explain why you would need to communicate with them.

6. Article 14 of the Universal Declaration of Human Rights (UDHR) says that everyone has the right to seek and enjoy asylum from persecution in other countries. Benjamin Zephaniah, a 12-year-old refugee boy, said 'This planet is for everyone, borders are for no one. It's all about freedom.' However, some countries have closed their borders to refugees. Give **two** reasons why countries might do this.

Ireland to evacuate!

Imagine there has been a nuclear catastrophe in Wales. As a result, Ireland must be totally abandoned. Vietnam has decided to accept 5,000 Irish refugees. You are the chairperson of the Vietnamese Resettlement Committee. It is the committee's job to make arrangements for welcoming the refugees from Ireland and for organising support for the next seven years.

You must decide the following.

1. Who will be on the Resettlement Committee? Give reasons for your answer.

   _____
   _____
   _____
   _____
   _____

2. What special needs will the refugees from Ireland have? (Consider some of the following: where they will live, language, work, education, welfare benefits, health, culture, contact with each other, religious practice.)

   _____
   _____
   _____
   _____
   _____

3. What things need to be done immediately to be ready for the refugees?

   _____
   _____
   _____
   _____
   _____

Travellers

I was hungry and you blamed it on my parents;

I was thirsty and you went to see the EEC wine lake;

I was sick and you told me to wait;

I was dying and you set up a Commission on Itinerancy,

A Review Body on Travellers, a Monitoring Body on what?

I was naked and you said so were my ancestors;

I had no job and you said we don't employ knackers;

I was all these things and you said it was the will of God;

I was homeless and you sent me a lorry load of stones and a bulldozer;

When did I see you hungry?

Margaret Maughan

1. Make a list of all the ways that the human dignity of Travellers is being denied in this poem.

    _____

    _____

    _____

    _____

    _____

    _____

2. Imagine you have invited the above poet to visit your school. Write the speech of welcome that you would give.

    _____

    _____

    _____

    _____

    _____

    _____

    _____

    _____

    _____

3. Write out **three** questions you would ask the poet about the life of a Traveller.

    (a) _____

    (b) _____

    (c) _____

The World Book of Children's Rights

FOLENS
Wellbeing

1. What are these drawings based on?

_____

_____

_____

2. What **four** priorities should be given to children, according to this poster?

_____

_____

_____

_____

3. What rights does the poster say all children have?

_____

_____

_____

_____

_____

_____

_____

_____

_____

_____

4. Pick any **four** children's rights and design your own symbols/pictures to go with them.

5. Describe **two** activities that the **Irish government** could organise to make sure that the voices and opinions of young people are heard.

(a) _____

_____

(b) _____

_____

Reema's story

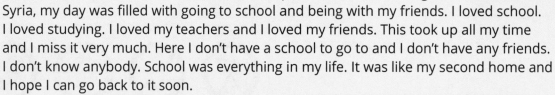

Hi! My name is Reema and I am 12 years old. I come from Syria but there has been a lot of fighting there, so my parents brought my brothers, my sister and me to live in northern Lebanon where it's safer. Our house in Lebanon is not very good because it's only half built and we have a very basic toilet and bathroom with no running water in it.

I don't have any activities during the day. The only thing I have now is to write and draw when I have a notebook and pens. When I was living in Syria, my day was filled with going to school and being with my friends. I loved school. I loved studying. I loved my teachers and I loved my friends. This took up all my time and I miss it very much. Here I don't have a school to go to and I don't have any friends. I don't know anybody. School was everything in my life. It was like my second home and I hope I can go back to it soon.

Now, I stay at home with my brothers and sister. We stay inside for most of the day. I have three brothers. They are aged ten, seven and two. I just have one sister. She's nine and we get on well. Back in Syria we had hens and doves but we have nothing here. We don't have running water like we did at home. We have to go to a spring nearby to collect water. We don't know if it's clean or not.

There is a song called 'Tomorrow will be better' and I like to sing that and I write poems, which I sometimes turn into songs. I used to enjoy writing before, but since coming here, after this tragedy, I have to write, I need to write. I couldn't stop writing even if I wanted to. The sadness drives me to write all the time. Here is a verse of one of my poems ...

Syria, we love you with all our hearts

Your children long to see you

We will never forget you

We will be back one day to wipe the tears off your cheeks

Source: *Oxfam*

1. What rights are being denied to Reema?

    _____

    _____

    _____

2. What do you think is the hardest thing for Reema to live with now?

    _____

    _____

    _____

3. Is Reema looking forward to going home? Explain your answer.

    _____

    _____

    _____

Child wanted

STREET WORKERS. MACHINE OPERATORS. MINEWORKERS. SCRAP-METAL COLLECTORS.

These are some of the most dangerous jobs you can imagine; yet children all over the world are being forced to do them, just to make enough money to survive.

As you read this, heavy machinery could be crushing a child's bones. Scraps of metal might be slashing a child's fingers. And a child on the street might be forced to sell their body for sex.

We don't need to tell you this is wrong.

Maurice lives in Nairobi, Kenya. He's eight. Every day he sifts through waste on rubbish dumps, looking for scraps of metal he can sell. Among the debris are shards of broken glass, steel nails and used needles. A single cut could lead to a life-threatening infection.

Maurice had a friend he used to work with on the dumps. While rooting around in the rubbish, this boy picked up a live wire and was killed instantly by the electrical charge it carried.

Maurice faces danger like this every single day. It's no life for a child. And it's why UNICEF is working tirelessly to help him and children like him.

When you have studied the leaflet, answer the following questions.

1. Which organisation produced this leaflet?

    _____

2. Name a job that children as young as four years of age are doing.

    _____

3. How old are some child scrap-metal collectors?

    _____

4. Name **five** different types of work in which child labourers are involved.

    _____

    _____

    _____

    _____

    _____

5. According to the story, what dangers does Maurice face?

    _____

    _____

    _____

6. The Protection of Young Persons (Employment) Act, 1996 states that the maximum
    weekly working hours are 0 hours for 14 year olds and 8 hours for 15 year olds during
    school term-time and 35 hours per week during holidays. Give **one** reason why you
    think this law was brought in.

    _____

    _____

    _____

    _____

7. The International Labour Organisation estimates that 246 million children between
    the ages of 5 and 17 years of age are working as child labourers. Most of these children
    are in Asia (60 per cent) and in Africa (32 per cent). Suggest **one** action **the Irish
    government** could take to help reduce the number of child labourers.

    _____

    _____

    _____

    _____

8. As a citizen of Ireland you can also play a role. Suggest **one** action **you** could take to
    inform people in your community about child labour.

    _____

    _____

    _____

    _____

Bullying

1. What is bullying? Fill in the speech bubbles.

2. Choose **one** of the actions listed here and describe how your **CSPE class** could get involved in it.

Have an anti-bullying week.	Go online and get information on bullying and make a display.	Run an anti-bullying poster campaign.
Have an anti-bullying assembly.	**What would you like your school to do?**	Invite a guest speaker on bullying.
Lobby your Student Council to get a policy on bullying.	Set up a support service for victims of bullying.	Write a song or poem to highlight bullying.

Action chosen: _____

Description: _____

_____

_____

_____

_____

_____

_____

_____

_____

_____

_____

I'm watching you!

Texting is a great way to stay in touch with your friends and family but sadly it can also be used to bully, harass and frighten people. Text bullying can be texts that frighten, insult, threaten or make you feel uncomfortable. **Your CSPE class** has decided to do some work on this issue.

1. Name and describe **three** other actions that **your school** could take to help prevent text bullying in your school.

    _____

    _____

    _____

    _____

    _____

2. Name an action that **your CSPE class** could undertake on this issue and describe **three** tasks your class would do as part of this action.

    _____

    _____

    _____

    _____

    _____

3. Write a short article for your school newsletter in which you give **three** pieces of advice about what students should do if they receive a bullying text message.

    _____

    _____

    _____

    _____

    _____

    _____

    _____

    _____

LGBT people

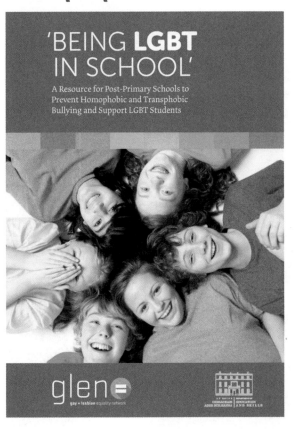

'BEING **LGBT** IN SCHOOL'

A Resource for Post-Primary Schools to Prevent Homophobic and Transphobic Bullying and Support LGBT Students

glen=
gay + lesbian equality network

FOLENS
Wellbeing

1. What do the letters LGBT stand for?

    _____

    _____

    _____

    _____

    _____

    _____

    _____

2. Why were these Guidelines produced?

    _____

    _____

    _____

    _____

    _____

    _____

    _____

3. What **two** organisations produced these Guidelines?

    _____

    _____

4. What supports does your school have in place for LGBT students?

    _____

    _____

    _____

    _____

    _____

    _____

    _____

    _____

5. Suggest **two actions** that your **class** could take to raise awareness of the supports available in your school for students who are LGBT.

    _____

    _____

    _____

    _____

    _____

Mastermind: your subject is human rights

1. Name one human right. _____

2. Name a country that denies its people some human rights. _____

3. Name a film about human rights. _____

4. Name a defender of human rights. _____

5. Name a human right that has been denied to children in the past. _____

    _____

6. Name an event in history that was a denial of human rights. _____

    _____

7. Name a song about human rights. _____

8. Name a right that has been denied to women in the past. _____

    _____

9. Name a poem about human rights. _____

10. Name a human rights organisation. _____

11. Name a right that has been denied to people of colour. _____

    _____

12. Name a human rights instrument. _____

Make a human rights tree

Now that you have studied human rights use all that you have learned to make a human rights tree using the template below. Use your textbook to help you complete it.

- Put leaves and flowers on the tree with the name of important human rights on them.

- Put roots on the tree to show what human rights need to grow and blossom (e.g. the instruments, a just society, people who will fight for rights, a good fair legal system).

- Put in a sun and rain drops with the names of the organisations that help human rights to stay healthy.

You could make a very large tree like this for your classroom wall or school corridor.

It would look great on 10 December which is International Human Rights Day.

Interview with a human rights activist

Choose any human rights activist (living or dead) from Chapter 3 of *Make A Difference!* and imagine that he or she is coming on a visit to your school. You are going to interview this person.

1. Write out **four** questions that you would ask your visitor.

Questions
A. _____
B. _____
C. _____
D. _____

2. Over the next few years, you might invite many speakers to talk to you about CSPE issues, so design the cover of a Visitors' Book for your classroom.

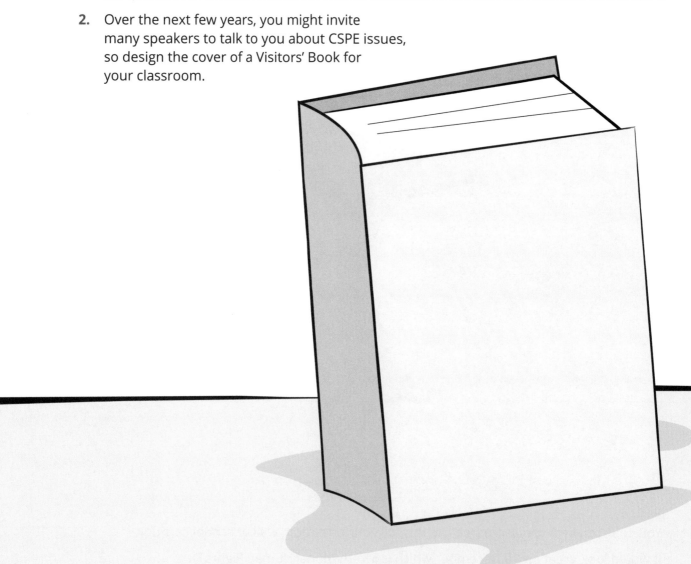

Social responsibilities

Overview of social responsibilities

Rights and responsibility go hand in hand and the citizen has certain responsibilities as well as having rights. Responsible citizens are thoughtful; they are aware of the issues in society. They understand and are willing to help overcome problems across a range of areas. Responsible citizens are generous; they are concerned with the rights of others and while caring for their own interests, they are willing to become involved in society for the common good. They know that society is better off when citizens do this.

A responsibility is something that it is your duty to do or to look after. For example, as a citizen, you have the right and the responsibility to vote, or you may be given the responsibility to sit on a jury deciding the innocence or guilt of another citizen.

Understanding how responsibility works in society is important. For example, employers have responsibilities to their employees, and the employees have responsibilities to their employers. Teachers and students have responsibilities to each other, the state has responsibility for its citizens. Responsibility is not a heavy load to carry – it is a freedom that you can enjoy as a citizen.

At this moment and as you are getting older, you will be in a position to make responsible choices that show you understand the power you have to make a difference. While you have responsibilities in lots of different areas of your life and many of these are about your personal wellbeing, others are about you helping to make the world a better place.

Studying CSPE is concerned with learning about both your rights as a young citizen and about your responsibilities too.

What would a responsible citizen do?

Write down what you could do in each situation below to show that you are a responsible citizen.

1. At a supermarket, you see a person pushing a buggy while carrying lots of shopping bags. They are trying to open the door to leave the shop. Explain what a responsible citizen would do.

   _____

   _____

   _____

   _____

2. It is your lucky day. You actually got a seat this morning on the bus! As you are going along, an older person gets on. There are no seats left. What would a responsible citizen do?

   _____

   _____

   _____

   _____

3. As Pat is walking down the hallway with a stack of books, Fran comes from behind and purposefully bumps into him. Pat stumbles and falls and his books go flying in all directions. Your classmates begin to laugh. What would a responsible citizen do?

   _____

   _____

   _____

   _____

Are you a responsible citizen?

Complete the questionnaire below and discuss your answers with **one** other student in your class.

		Yes	Sometimes	Never
1.	Do you obey the laws of the country?	Yes	Sometimes	Never
2.	Do you respect Garda authority?	Yes	Sometimes	Never
3.	Do you draw graffiti on walls?	Yes	Sometimes	Never
4.	Do you always follow the school rules?	Yes	Sometimes	Never
5.	Do you throw litter on the ground?	Yes	Sometimes	Never
6.	Do you reduce, reuse and recycle?	Yes	Sometimes	Never
7.	Do you help your neighbours?	Yes	Sometimes	Never
8.	Do you fight with people?	Yes	Sometimes	Never
9.	Do you co-operate with your classmates?	Yes	Sometimes	Never
10.	Do you take things belonging to others?	Yes	Sometimes	Never

> **Don't ever forget that you're a citizen of this world, and there are things you can do to lift the human spirit, things that are easy, things that are free, things that you can do every day. Civility, respect, kindness, character.**
>
> Aaron Sorkin

What do the following words mean:

(a) Civility _____

(b) Respect _____

(c) Kindness _____

(d) Character _____

Who is responsible?

Look at each of the broken items numbered 1 to 8 and answer the following questions for each item:

(a) Why was this item useful?

(b) Who might be affected because it is broken?

(c) Who has the responsibility to do something about it?

1.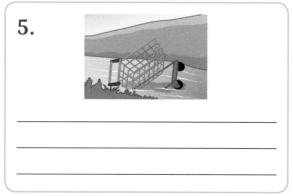

_____

_____

_____

2.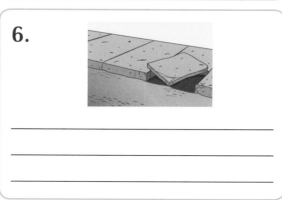

_____

_____

_____

3.

_____

_____

_____

4.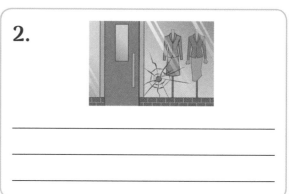

_____

_____

_____

5.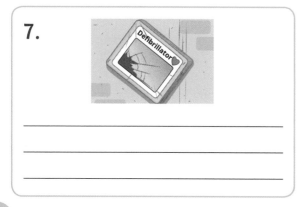

_____

_____

_____

6.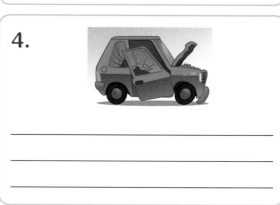

_____

_____

_____

7.

_____

_____

_____

8.

_____

_____

_____

The state's responsibilities to its citizens

Imagine that you are a member of a new state that has just become independent. You have been asked to help draw up a new charter or constitution for this state. What responsibility will this new state have towards its citizens?

Below are some of the areas for which you will be responsible. Rank them by putting a number in front of each of them, 1 being the most important responsibility of the state and 20 being the least important. Give a reason for your ranking beside each area. Discuss your ranking with a group of classmates.

Newlandia

Rank	Area	Reason
	Security	
	Justice	
	Education	
	Law and order	
	Equality	
	Employment	
	Happiness	
	Peace	
	Healthcare	
	Social welfare	
	Basic human needs such as food, shelter and clothing	
	Taxation	
	Sign agreements with other countries	
	Public works (roads, parks, bridges and rivers)	
	Water	
	Power/energy	
	Defence (army, navy and air force)	
	National language and heritage	
	Development	
	Culture and the arts	

Making choices

Read the following statements and decide which option you would like best.

FOLENS
Wellbeing

I would prefer to:

1. Take part in a student v teacher football match to fundraise ☐
2. Take part in a student v teacher quiz to fundraise ☐
3. Take part in a student v teacher basketball match to fundraise ☐

I would prefer to:

1. Visit the Dáil ☐
2. Visit a courthouse ☐
3. Visit the county council offices ☐

I would prefer to:

1. Meet the President of Ireland ☐
2. Meet the Taoiseach ☐
3. Meet my local TD ☐

I would prefer to:

1. Live in a city ☐
2. Live in the country ☐
3. Live in a small town ☐

I would prefer to:

1. Write an article for the school magazine ☐
2. Take part in a debate ☐
3. Be interviewed ☐

I would prefer to:

1. Look after sick people ☐
2. Take care of animals ☐
3. Volunteer abroad to help the poor ☐

I would prefer to:

1. Clean up the school ☐
2. Clean up the local area ☐
3. Clean up the park ☐

How do you make decisions?

_____

_____

_____

_____

My **RESPONSIBILITY** poem

Complete this poem using the letters from the word RESPONSIBILITY as your guide.

R is for responsibility, the other side of rights

E is for _____

S is for _____

P is for _____

O is for _____

N is for _____

S is for _____

I is for _____

B is for _____

I is for _____

L is for _____

I is for _____

T is for _____

Y is for _____

Responsible pet owners

Toby the terrier said, 'I know what I want for Christmas. I want a child.'

'You're not getting a child and that's that!' barked Mrs Terrier. 'How many times do I have to tell you? It costs too much money to keep a child. We can't afford one.'

'Ah, Mam, let him get a child,' said Mimi, Toby's sister. 'A cute little child, with bright eyes and curly hair.'

'No, no,' said Mrs Terrier. 'A child has to be looked after and fed. It needs exercise and attention. I know who would end up doing it all – me, as usual! You have no idea what a can of people food costs these days. You can't just feed them on scraps, you know. Who'll mind the child when we go away, I ask you?'

'The Sheepdog family down the road have two fully grown people,' whined Toby.

'The Sheepdogs are better off than we are. You can't have a child just because they have one.'

Mimi began to whimper a little and Mrs Terrier said, 'Well, okay, I'll talk to your father when he gets in, but don't go building your hopes up. Now go and watch *Paw Patrol* on TV.'

1. What responsibilities did Mrs Terrier point out to Toby and Mimi about having a child pet?

    _____

    _____

    _____

2. How is the story like a child wanting to get a puppy?

    _____

    _____

    _____

3. Give this story a different title.

    _____

I don't think we should keep animals as pets. I think all animals should live in the wild. It's wrong to put birds in cages or keep fish in bowls or tanks or to lock up dogs and cats in houses all day long. All animals should be free, like us.

You're wrong. Children can learn a lot from pets. They can learn how pets feed, mate, grow and die. If they have a pet to look after, they learn how to look after a living thing. Pets are company for people living alone. It's fair to animals, too, because some animals like to live with humans. Tame animals wouldn't be able to survive in the wild.

4. What do you think?

    _____

    _____

    _____

Know Your Neighbour weekend

The Know Your Neighbour campaign has been set up to encourage people to organise an activity and to invite their neighbours to do it. You and some of your friends have decided to organise an event in your neighbourhood to help your neighbours to get to know one another.

(a) Design an invitation that you would send to each of your neighbours, inviting them to your special Know Your Neighbour event. You should include in your invitation at least **three** pieces of key information that your neighbours would need to know.

(b) State and explain **three** reasons why you think this campaign is important for people in your neighbourhood.

_____

_____

_____

_____

_____

(c) Apart from the invitation, describe in detail **two** actions that you and your friends could take in order to promote this Know Your Neighbour event.

_____

_____

_____

_____

_____

_____

_____

Strand 01 Review

In this strand, you learned about:

- Human rights and human rights instruments ☐
- Human rights issues such as disability, rights of older people, travellers' rights, bullying, LGBT people's rights, child labour and homelessness ☐
- Prejudice, discrimination, stereotyping and equality ☐

- Asylum seekers, displaced people and refugees ☐
- Human rights activists and organisations ☐
- Social responsibilities ☐
- Responsibility in action ☐

And you carried out an action ☐

Look back over the lessons and activities that you have completed. In the table below, tick the skills that you may have used or learned.

Managing myself	Staying well	Managing information and thinking	Being numerate
I know myself better ☐	I am healthy and active ☐	I was curious ☐	I expressed ideas mathematically ☐
I made decisions ☐	I am social ☐	I gathered and analysed information ☐	I estimated, predicted and calculated ☐
I set goals ☐	I am safe ☐	I thought creatively ☐	I was interested in problem-solving ☐
I achieved goals ☐	I feel confident ☐	I thought about what I learned ☐	I saw patterns and trends ☐
I thought about what I learned ☐	I feel positive about what I learned ☐	I used digital technology to access, manage and share information ☐	I gathered and presented data using digital technology to review and understand numbers ☐
I used technology to learn ☐			

Being creative	Working with others	Communicating	Being literate
I used my imagination ☐	I developed relationships ☐	I used language ☐	I understand some new words ☐
I thought about things from a different point of view ☐	I dealt with conflict ☐	I used numbers ☐	I enjoyed words and language ☐
I put ideas into action ☐	I co-operated ☐	I listened to my classmates ☐	I wrote for different reasons ☐
I learned in a creative way ☐	I respected difference ☐	I expressed myself ☐	I expressed my ideas clearly ☐
I was creative with digital technology ☐	I helped make the world a better place ☐	I performed/ presented ☐	I developed my spoken language ☐
	I learned with others ☐	I had a discussion/ debate ☐	I read and wrote in different ways ☐
	I worked with others using digital technology ☐	I used technology to communicate ☐	

Now write down two skills from the list that you think you should focus on more in the future.

_____

Our developing world

Overview of our developing world

Development and change are all around us. Ask anybody in Ireland and they will tell you just how much Ireland has developed recently, with new roads, buildings, businesses, factories, houses, apartments, new types of transport, more computers, broadband, smart phones and technology. However, when it comes to development and planning, sometimes people have different points of view.

Around the world, countries are changing and developing. In some places the change is rapid, while in others it is much slower. Some places are called 'developing countries' because their development is at a slower pace compared to more developed states. Some of these countries have problems that are linked to famine, poverty, natural disasters and corrupt leaders.

Much development is planned. Governments, local authorities and communities spend a lot of time planning for successful development, which lasts into the future, and development that is good for the planet. There are plans too for world development; one of them is called the Sustainable Development Goals (SDGs). The 17 SDGs are the way in which many countries around the world are trying to make the world a better, fairer and more equal place for all.

Development usually means change for the better, but when you study this area you will learn that this is not always the case. Poverty is a real issue in the lives of people here in Ireland; and extreme poverty is faced by many people in different parts of the world. Poverty makes sustainable development very difficult, so finding just ways of overcoming poverty is a big challenge for the world.

Developing Ireland

Starting with the earliest development listed below, put the date in the signpost and write beside it which development happened in Ireland in that year.

1973   Ireland joined the EU.

2002   Eircom began rolling out broadband internet access.

1946   Rural electrification began (bringing electricity to all parts of the country).

1967   Free second level education was introduced.

1999   Ireland started using the euro.

1949   Ireland became a republic.

2004   Free medical cards were given to the over 70s.

1876   The first telephone was used in Ireland.

1960   Telefís Éireann began broadcasting as the first national TV station.

1926   Radio Éireann was set up.

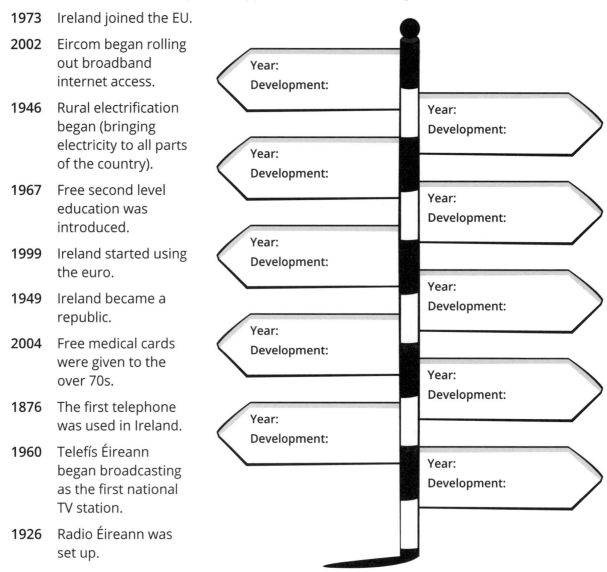

From the list above, choose the development that you think was the most important one and explain why you have chosen it.

Development: _____

Reason: _____

_____

_____

_____

_____

_____

_____

Tips for doing an interview

Interviewer's name: _____   Date: _____

Person being interviewed: _____

Person's age: _____

Place of birth: _____

Other places lived in: _____

Number of brothers and sisters: _____

What did your parents do? _____

What is the earliest memory that you have? _____

_____

_____

What was school like when you were young? Was it the same for boys and girls?

_____

_____

What games did you play? _____

How old were you when you left school? _____

What did you do then? _____

_____

_____

What is the best invention that has happened in your lifetime?

_____

Tell me why you picked this?

_____

_____

Time capsule

Imagine you are going to bury a time capsule in your school (or back garden), so that people in the future can see what developments have happened. Its contents should show people in 2100 what life was like in Ireland this year.

1. What 10 items would you select to bury? Why?

ITEM	REASON

2. When you have made your list, compare it with one other person in your class. Then agree 10 items between you.

3. Write a note that you would put into the time capsule for the person opening it in 2100.

_____

_____

_____

_____

_____

_____

_____

_____

_____

_____

_____

_____

My world in the year 2060

Tom Odhiambo (16), Kenya

In 2060 I will be a farmer. I will have a dip and fences for my cattle. I will have crop rotation and fertilisers. I hope to do a lot for the country so everyone will have a lot of food.

Tracy Cernan (15), US

I do not ever want to be broke. I will need to get a good job to earn enough money to keep the lifestyle I have grown up with. I guess by 2060 the US will be even more rich and powerful.

Valerie Bouget (15), France

My feather alarm tickles my feet. I get up and my robot, Gaston, serves breakfast. Electronic life is okay, but boring. I take my helicopter to work and check that the orders I gave yesterday are obeyed.

Asanatu Koroma (14), Sierra Leone

The houses will be made of stone. They will cost €500 and will last a long time. The roads will be made of tar. There will not be any beggars or poor people. Everyone will have jobs and food.

1. How do the future views of the four young people differ?

_____

_____

_____

_____

_____

_____

2. Imagine that you are 90 years old, looking back at your life. What developments do you think will have taken place so that you will think of now as the 'good old days'?

_____

_____

_____

_____

_____

_____

_____

_____

_____

_____

_____

_____

Planning a community centre for Ballyouth

Ballyouth Council agreed last week that they were going to build a new community centre. Councillor Breda O'Reilly said, 'It's about time some money was spent on the youth of our town. Young people today don't have enough to do. That's why they turn to vandalism, drugs and crime.' The community centre will have a swimming pool and sports hall for badminton, table tennis and weight training. At the moment, the nearest swimming pool is in Ballyolder, 10 km away. Ballyouth Community School opens their sports hall to the public, but only during the evenings and at weekends. Councillor O'Reilly said she would be interested to hear the views of young people in the area.

Ciara O'Brien: I have a moped. I think the money should be spent on a workshop so we can learn to mend our bikes.

Jessica Kelly: I think the council should build a snooker hall. Snooker is very popular with young people here.

Rebecca Harrington: At the moment, there's nothing for young people to do in Ballyouth, so we wander around the shopping centre. I think we need somewhere to go where we can chat and have a cup of coffee.

Jimmy Kennedy: Most of my friends spend their time playing in the arcades. What we need is somewhere else to go. I think Ballyouth needs a skating rink.

Kevin Sweeney: I think there's too much money spent on sport. I hate sport. I think young people in Ballyouth need somewhere to have a disco.

Write an email to Councillor O'Reilly to tell her what you think of her plan. Use the ideas above and add any ideas of your own.

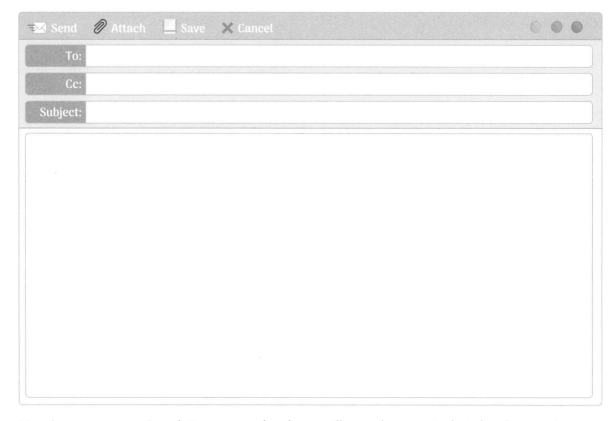

Now in your copy write a letter to your local councillor and suggest what developments might be good for your local community.

Motorway development

The National Roads Authority (NRA) has announced that a new motorway is to be built. The route chosen crosses an area where important wildlife will be threatened. You and members of your community have decided to campaign for a different route for the new motorway.

1. Write a letter to your local councillor objecting to the planned route through this important environmental area. In your letter make **three** arguments against the route that has been chosen.

    (a) _____
    _____
    _____

    (b) _____
    _____
    _____

    (c) _____
    _____
    _____

2. Apart from letter writing, describe **three** actions your community could take as part of the campaign to get a different route for the motorway.

    (a) _____
    _____
    _____

    (b) _____
    _____
    _____

    (c) _____
    _____
    _____

3. Name and explain **two** skills that you would use while campaigning against the proposed motorway development.

    (a) _____
    _____
    _____

    (b) _____
    _____
    _____

Poster for Rio +30

The year is now 2022! Create a poster advertising Rio +30. Include the issues that might feature on the agenda. Make sure to include an image and a slogan in your poster.

SDG connections

Goal 1   No poverty

Goal 2   No hunger

Goal 3   Good health

Goal 4   Quality education

Goal 5   Gender equality

Goal 6   Clean water and sanitation

Goal 7   Renewable energy

Goal 8   Good jobs and economic growth

Goal 9   Innovation and infrastructure

Goal 10 Reduced inequalities

Goal 11 Sustainable cities and communities

Goal 12 Responsible consumption

Goal 13 Climate action

Goal 14 Life below water

Goal 15 Life on land

Goal 16 Peace and justice

Goal 17 Partnerships for the goals

(a) Now that you know about the 17 Sustainable Development Goals (SDGs), connect each goal with its corresponding icon/logo.

(b) Which goals, do you think, are most important for children and young people? List your top **five** goals in order of priority.

1. _____

2. _____

3. _____

4. _____

5. _____

(c) List **one** goal that you are prepared to work on. Explain how you are going to do this.

_____

_____

_____

Measuring development

Having explored the countries with 'Very high Human Development' and 'Low Human Development' in your textbook, now look at the countries who are in the middle. Write down 10 questions you could ask about the countries and the figures below in your copy. Then give them to a classmate to answer.

High human development

Rank		Country	HDI	
2015 estimates for 2014	Change in rank from previous year		2015 estimates for 2014	Change from previous year
50	▲ (1)	Belarus	0.798	▲ 0.002
50	—	Russia	0.798	▲ 0.001
52	—	Oman	0.793	▲ 0.001
52	▲ (1)	Romania	0.793	▲ 0.002
52	▲ (2)	Uruguay	0.793	▲ 0.003
55	—	Bahamas	0.790	▲ 0.004
56	—	Kazakhstan	0.788	▲ 0.003
57	▼ (1)	Barbados	0.785	—
58	—	Antigua and Barbadu	0.783	▲ 0.002

Medium human development

Rank		Country	HDI	
2015 estimates for 2014	Change in rank from previous year		2015 estimates for 2014	Change from previous year
106	—	Botswana	0.698	▲ 0.002
107	—	Moldova	0.693	▲ 0.003
108	—	Egypt	0.690	▲ 0.001
109	—	Turkmenistan	0.688	▲ 0.006
110	▲ (1)	Gabon	0.684	▲ 0.005
110	—	Indonesia	0.684	▲ 0.003
112	▲ (1)	Paraguay	0.679	▲ 0.002
113	▼ (2)	Palestine	0.677	▼ 0.002
114	—	Uzbekistan	0.675	▲ 0.003
115	—	Philippines	0.668	▲ 0.004
116	▼ (1)	El Salvador	0.666	▲ 0.002
116	▲ (1)	South Africa	0.666	▲ 0.003
116	▲ (1)	Vietnam	0.666	▲ 0.003

The poverty cycle

It is a myth that there is a culture of poverty and that all poor people are the same. However, some people get caught in what is called a poverty cycle or poverty trap. Below is a poverty cycle.

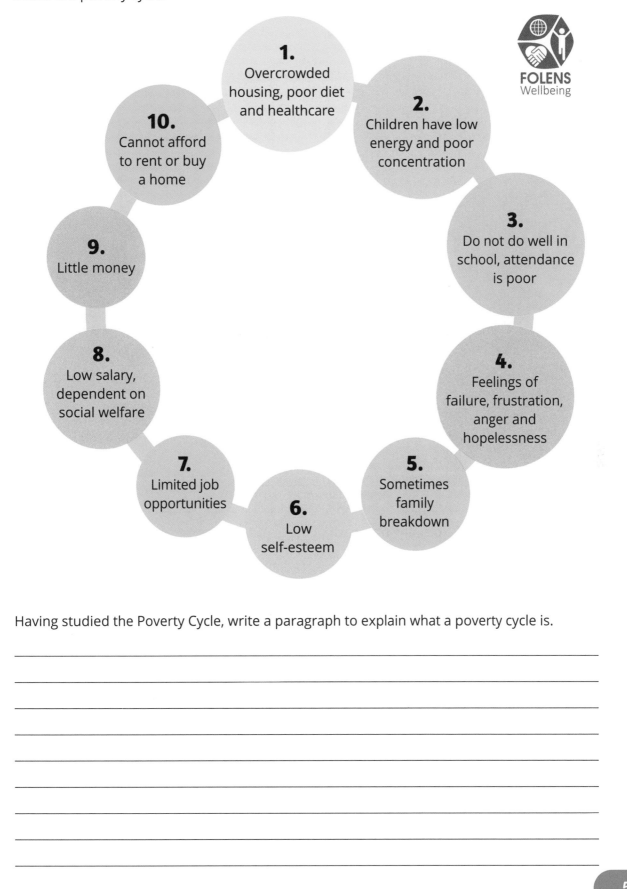

Having studied the Poverty Cycle, write a paragraph to explain what a poverty cycle is.

_____

_____

_____

_____

_____

_____

_____

_____

_____

Overcoming poverty

Look at the cartoon and identify **four** ways in which people can overcome poverty.

1. _____ 3. _____

2. _____ 4. _____

Write a few sentences explaining how each of these can help people to overcome poverty.

1. _____

_____

_____

2. _____

_____

_____

3. _____

_____

_____

4. _____

_____

_____

Poverty wordle

Using the words you associate with poverty, create your own wordle. The word POVERTY has to stand out as the largest and clearest word so you should put it in first.

06 Sustainable living

Overview of sustainable living

Learning about being a good citizen is also about learning to care for our environment by living sustainably. Sustainable living is about taking our responsibility for the environment seriously. It means that we have responsibility for the world for the years we live on the Earth and that it is up to us to pass this Earth on, in a healthy state, to the next generations. Over time, the planet has suffered and many problems are facing the world today. Issues like climate change, greenhouse gases, holes in the ozone layer and global warming are often in the news.

The problems facing the Earth are big issues for governments and many laws are passed to try to protect the world. For example, governments have environmental policies on waste and carbon emissions. National groups like Tidy Towns, An Taisce, ECO-UNESCO and Friends of the Earth are devoted to the care and protection of the Irish environment.

In local communities, people work together to care for the environment – Green Schools are set up, Tidy Town committees work hard to keep areas tidy, and other local groups like residents' associations work to make areas look clean and cared for.

But sustainable living is the responsibility of every individual – you can play your part in caring for planet Earth. How? It might surprise you to learn that the things you do, like dropping litter or using certain sprays, can affect the whole world. You can also care for the environment by using your power as a consumer (buyer of goods), such as choosing things with less packaging or packaging that can be recycled, and by being responsible in the ways you dispose of things once they are used up or you no longer need them. This is when you can choose to reuse, to reduce and to recycle. Years ago, things were made to last for a long time, but now we live in a world where things are disposable and have a short lifespan. So, we are creating more and more waste.

Animals are part of our environment and we have a duty to care for and protect them. We also have to respect their rights and make sure that we do not cause them harm or suffering, or cause them to become extinct by our actions. Being a guardian of the planet is one responsibility of being a good citizen.

Earth damage podcast

Divide into six small groups. Each group should read **one** Earth Damage Report on pages 156 and 157 of *Make A Difference!* and then prepare a podcast on this topic using the Earth Damage Report's information. Then you should perform your piece for the class.

Programme introduction:

_____

_____

_____

_____

_____

_____

Title of piece of music or poem: _____

Time: _____

Why was this piece chosen?

_____

_____

_____

_____

_____

Name of person you have chosen to interview: _____

Why you have chosen this person? _____

_____

_____

_____

_____

_____

What this person has to say about the theme of your Earth Damage Report: _____

_____

_____

_____

_____

_____

_____

Environmental poems
Great Green Limericks

There was a young man from Brazil
Who cut down the trees on a hill.
It rained all one day
And the soil washed away
So life on the hill now is nil.

Now write your own limerick:

_____

_____

_____

_____

The Newcomer

'There's something new in the river,'
The fish said as it swam.
'It's got no scales, no fins, no gills.
And ignores the impassable dam.'

'There's something new in the trees.'
I heard a bloated thrush sing,
'It's got no beak, no claws, no feathers,
And not even the ghost of a wing.'

'There's something new in the warren,'
The rabbit said to the doe,
'It's got no fur, no eyes, no paws.
Yet digs deeper than we can go.'

'There's something new in the whiteness.'
Said the snow-bright polar bear,
'I saw its shadow on a glacier
But it left no footprints there.'

Throughout the animal kingdom
The news was spreading fast –

No beak, no claws, no feathers,
No scales, no fur, no gills,
It lives in the trees and the water.
In the earth and the snow and the hills,
And it kills and it kills and it kills.

'The Newcomer' from *Gargling With Jelly* by
Brian Patten. Published by Puffin, 1986.

1.   Name the different creatures mentioned in the poem.

_____

_____

2.   What is 'The Newcomer'?

_____

_____

A litter-free zone

You are the local Litter Warden. Write a reply to each of these local residents below.

For goodness' sake, tractors drop muck everywhere. They can't help it. I don't know what all the fuss is about.

I have three children. You can't expect me to be responsible if they drop sweet papers on the ground. I've got plenty of other things to worry about.

No one can take away my right to throw litter when and where I want! It's my right to do whatever I want.

(a) Farmer Frank   **(b)** Peter Parent   **(c)** Roger Right

Life's too short to worry about litter. Putting litter in a bin is just too much of an effort. Anyway, what difference do a few papers make?

After a fun day at the beach, who wants to pick up empty cans, sweet papers and dirty nappies? Sure, when the tide comes in, they'll all be washed out to sea anyway.

(d) Danielle Don't Care   **(e)** Sonia Sloppy

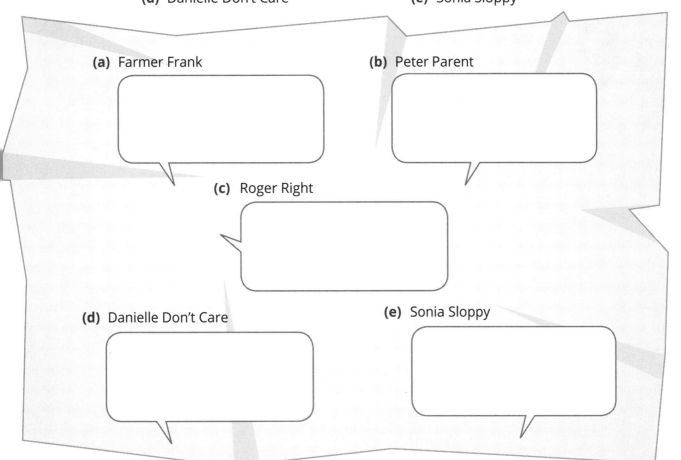

(a) Farmer Frank

(b) Peter Parent

(c) Roger Right

(d) Danielle Don't Care

(e) Sonia Sloppy

How long does litter last?

When you have studied the poster opposite, answer the following questions.

1. What is the overall message in this poster?

_____

_____

_____

_____

2. Which organisation produced this poster?

_____

3. List the litter items that will still be around in 100 years' time, according to this poster.

_____

_____

_____

_____

_____

4. What item on the list lasts the shortest amount of time before it disappears?

_____

_____

_____

_____

_____

5. What accounts for 60 per cent of all litter collected?

_____

_____

_____

_____

_____

6. According to the poster, what should you do with leftovers?

_____

_____

_____

_____

_____

7. What law makes littering an offence?

_____

_____

_____

_____

Jumble Town

FREE FURNITURE!

(and lots of other items for the home, workplace and school) available for collection in your local area from JumbleTown online.

Some of the items are new; most are good-quality second-hand.

You can also give away items on this eco-website. Its main aim is to promote the practice of life-cycling before costly recycling or disposal.

Jumble Town is good for you, the community and the environment.

Someone, somewhere wants it!

1. What is the main aim of Jumble Town?

    _____

    _____

    _____

    _____

2. What can you get at Jumble Town?

    _____

    _____

    _____

3. What is the slogan for Jumble Town?

    _____

4. Who benefits from Jumble Town?

    _____

    _____

    _____

5. How is Jumble Town good for the environment?

    _____

    _____

    _____

6. In your copy design a new poster to advertise Jumble Town.

The three Rs

Explain the **three** Rs and give examples below.

R1 _____

Explanation:

_____

_____

_____

_____

Examples:

_____

_____

_____

R2 _____

Explanation:

_____

_____

_____

_____

Examples:

_____

_____

_____

R3 _____

Explanation:

_____

_____

_____

_____

Examples:

_____

_____

_____

_____

Alternative energies

Complete the table below explaining how each type of energy works, and its advantages and disadvantages.

Type of energy	How it works	Advantages	Disadvantages
Water			
Solar			
Wind			
Nuclear			

Don't go to the animal circus campaign

The ISPCA believes that circuses cannot always provide enough space and proper conditions to guarantee the wellbeing of their animals. While circuses can be entertaining and great fun, they believe that animal circuses are cruel and unnecessary. You and members of your community have decided to protest to your local authority about the use of land in your area for the staging of a circus using animals.

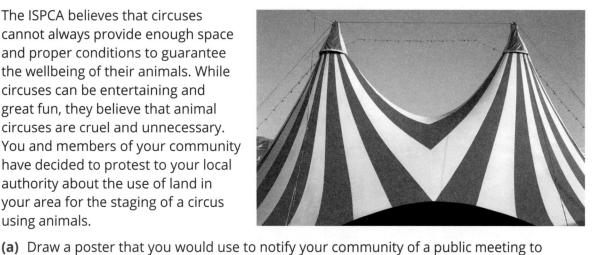

(a) Draw a poster that you would use to notify your community of a public meeting to be held to organise the protest. You should include a slogan referring to the Don't Go to the Animal Circus Campaign in your poster, with a drawing or picture.

(b) Describe the work of **three** committees that you would set up in order to organise your protest.

_____

_____

_____

_____

_____

(c) Write a note to your local council objecting to the staging of the animal circus in your area, suggesting **three** animal welfare reasons why this circus should not go ahead.

_____

_____

_____

_____

_____

Do animals have rights?

A chicken shed in a battery factory can hold up to 30,000 birds. They live there for about 50 days before they are killed for meat. There are often no windows in the shed. The light comes from dull bulbs. Big fans suck out the stale air in the summertime. Most of the birds sit quietly, stretching out a leg from time to time. The farmer watches the light all the time. If it gets too dark, the birds won't eat; if it gets too bright, the birds peck at each other. In fact, the farmer often doesn't even go into the shed. Heat, light and food are all controlled from outside the chicken shed.

1. In what way is battery farming cruel to animals?

    _____

    _____

    _____

2. As consumers of chickens and eggs, how do we benefit from battery farming?

    _____

    _____

    _____

3. Free range is the opposite of battery farming. What does 'free range' mean?

    _____

    _____

    _____

4. Do animals have rights? Explain your answer.

    _____

    _____

    _____

Animal rights: who is watching who?

This gorilla has lived for many years in a zoo. There are about 475 gorillas in captivity. Some zoos keep gorillas living in very poor, cramped conditions, but others have learned to provide very well for these animals. Some gorillas live for 40 years in zoos.

1. If this gorilla could speak, what would he say about people? Remember, all he would know about people would be what he had learned from being watched in the zoo.

    _____

    _____

    _____

2. What kind of animal could suffer most from being kept in a zoo?

    _____

    _____

3. If pets could talk, what would they say about people?

    _____

    _____

    _____

In Barcelona Zoo in Spain, a man was put into a cage to see how visitors would react to him. The man was told to do nothing special. He just behaved normally. He ate, washed, slept and so on. The funny thing was that people spent ages looking at him and seemed just as curious about this human being as they were about the other animals in the zoo.

4. Why do you think people did this?

    _____

    _____

5. What purpose do zoos serve?

    _____

    _____

    _____

Mother Earth Day

Senator Nelson, an American politician, thought of the idea of having a special day to do something about what is happening to the environment. The first Mother Earth Day happened in the US on 22 April 1970 and is now celebrated around the world on that date.

As part of your learning about sustainable development, your CSPE class has decided to get involved in Mother Earth Day.

(a) Draw a poster to raise awareness about Mother Earth Day. You should include a suitable slogan in your poster, with a drawing or picture.

(b) Describe **two** practical actions your CSPE class could take on Mother Earth Day to encourage people in your community to look after their environment.

_____

_____

_____

_____

_____

(c) Write a short piece for your school magazine explaining why Mother Earth Day is important. Give **two** different reasons for getting involved.

_____

_____

_____

_____

_____

Ivy and Caterpillars board game

Think about the good and bad things that people do in their gardens. Ivy and Caterpillars is a board game for two to four players just like Snakes and Ladders. There are two blank Ivy squares (2, 35) and two blank Caterpillar squares (21, 41) for you to fill in. Get some counters and a dice. Don't forget to play the game!

48 FINISH	**47**	**46**	45 You paint a fence with creosote	44	43
37	38	39	40	41	42
36	35	**34**	33	32	31 You cut down a tree and never replace it
25	26	27	28 You fill the composting bin	29	30
24 You use slug pellets	23 You weed the flowerbeds	22	**21**	20	19
13	14	15	16	17 You don't clean up your pet's waste	18 You collect water in a barrel for watering the plants
12	11	10	9	8	7
1 START	2	3	4	5 You prune trees to help them grow better	**6**

My green heart

Think about all that you have learned in this chapter on sustainable living and in your green heart below write in the following:

- What you love about the world in which you live.
- What your hope is for the world in which you live.
- One thing that you could do to help protect the environment for future generations.
- One thing that your own generation could do to protect the environment for the future.
- One thing that countries working together could do to protect the environment for the future.

FOLENS
Wellbeing

Signature: ....

Date: ....

COP21 infographic

An infographic is a way of putting words and pictures together to share information.

Use the information in Lesson 54 in your textbook to design your very own COP21 Key Points Infographic.

You can use a mind map, circles or other shapes with a small graphic, picture, drawing or image and then include the key information in simple language. You do not need to be brilliant at art to design an infographic!

07 Effecting global change

Overview of effecting global change

Global living describes the ways in which we are linked to other people and other countries worldwide. If you think about the food you eat, the clothes you wear and the things you have, you will quickly realise just how you are connected to places everywhere. If you lived outside of Ireland, you would discover that there are ways in which people from other countries are connected to us too.

Once you realise all the connections you have around the world, you can think about the choices you make. These choices affect people in distant places, such as the clothes you buy that are made in sweatshops, the shoes you wear that are made by child labour, the coffee you drink or the bananas you eat for which the farmer gets very little payment. You have the choice to make a difference and to buy wisely (for example, buying Fairtrade products) in order to be a responsible global citizen.

Some people think that linking people around the globe in many ways, called globalisation, is a wonderful development, while others believe that it is causing more and more inequality in the world.

Ireland is a small island at the edge of Europe, but it plays a big part on the global stage. Studying global living allows you to explore some of the many ways that Ireland is connected, and how you, as a young citizen, are a citizen of the world.

Interdependence

We live in an interdependent world, which means we are linked in many ways to other places. Examine this drawing and then locate on the map below all the places mentioned in it.

Dad's jumper
Made from cashmere wool from New Zealand

Mum's makeup
Celebrity-endorsed moisturiser from France

Website
Online site originating in Chile

Computer
Product of a major Chinese technologies company

Desk
Purchased from a major furniture retailer in Sweden

Printer
Product of a major American technologies company

Boy's shoes
Brand-named shoes made in an outsourced factory in India

Hand-held game
Product from a Taiwanese factory

Toy car
Distributed by the South African office of a Korean toy manufacturer

Girl's boots
Leather product from Argentina

Shopping bag
Purchased from a local franchise of a major clothing store in the UK

Laptop
Shipped from a local assembly plant in Munich

Girl's dress
Product of a global lifestyle clothing company in Canada

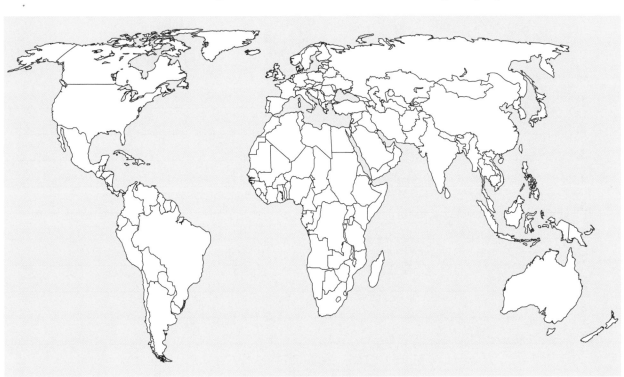

You could do this activity for a selection of things in your home too!

Global issues

Below are the global issues that face the world. Choose any 10 issues and write a sentence on each of them.

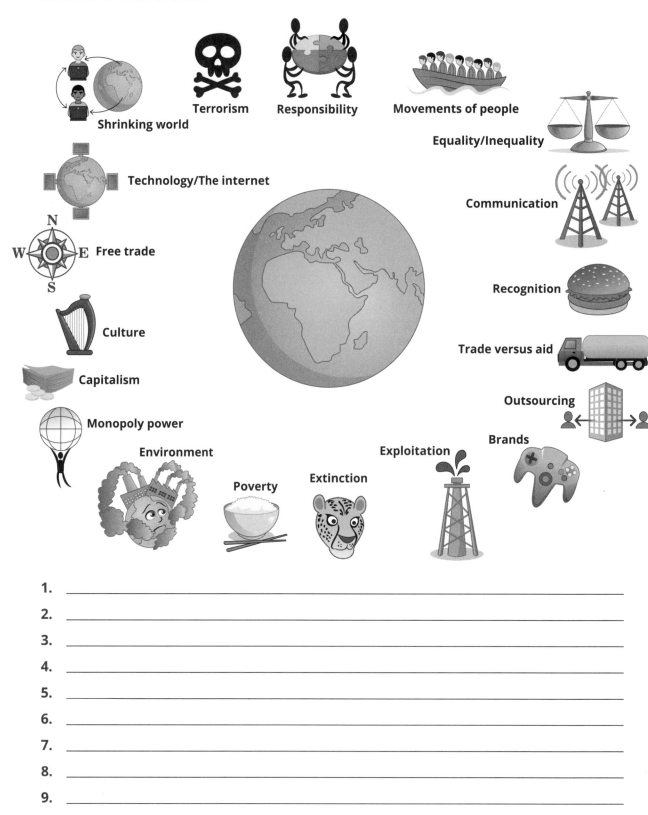

1. _____
2. _____
3. _____
4. _____
5. _____
6. _____
7. _____
8. _____
9. _____
10. _____

A postcard from Barbara

Imagine you are Barbara Banana and you want to send a card to a friend from one place on your life journey. Complete the front of the card with a suitable drawing or picture and then write a message and the address on the back.

Front of postcard

Back of postcard

POSTCARD

FOR ADDRESS ONLY

You choose …

When it comes to buying things, we all have choices to make. As with many choices, there are pros and cons. Think about the following issues that influence people when they buy food.

FOLENS
Wellbeing

Type of shopping	Cons
ORGANIC Some people want food that has no chemicals in it.	But …
COST Some people buy the cheapest food they can.	But …
LOCAL Some people like to support their local shopkeeper.	But …
CONVENIENCE Some people buy food wherever it is handy for them to shop.	But …
ENVIRONMENTAL Some people are very aware of the environment and buy food that has been grown locally. So, it has not travelled long distances, which causes pollution.	But …
FAIRTRADE Some consumers like to know that the people who produce the food are paid a fair price for it.	But …

Here is a list of cons. Put the correct letter in the column beside the issue connected to that type of shopping. You **can** use the same letter more than once.

(a) It costs a lot.

(b) It is not always convenient.

(c) Some places do not stock these goods.

(d) The food might not be organic.

(e) The food might not be fairly traded.

(f) The environment might have been damaged in producing these goods.

(g) The money made on selling these goods might not stay in the local area.

List some other cons here.

_____

_____

_____

_____

Change today, choose Fairtrade

Fairtrade Fortnight

Study the leaflet above and answer the following questions.

1. According to the leaflet, what is the message for Fairtrade Fortnight?

   _____

2. Name **three** countries where there are thousands of farmers living in poverty.

   (a) _____ **(b)** _____ **(c)** _____

3. What does the infographic on the leaflet tell us about children?

   _____

   _____

   _____

   _____

4. Copy the Fairtrade logo into the space provided.

In the right cup

Match the statement to the **correct** coffee cup.

A My workers could lose their job at any time.

B My workers work 11 hours a day, six days a week.

C My farmer has a guaranteed contract every year.

D My workers have poor homes, little chance of an education and poor health.

E I was grown on a plantation in South America. I was then sold to a big coffee company.

F My workers belong to a co-op and I will be processed there.

G I was bought by a coyote from the poor farmer who harvested me.

H My workers have good homes and a decent standard of living.

I My farmer uses chemicals and pesticides to grow me.

J I was grown and then a broker bought me.

K I was never bought by a middleman.

L I was grown on a small farm in South America. I was then sold to a Fairtrade company.

Technology in our lives survey

Carry out this survey with 10 people. Be sure to ask people of different ages.

Turn the information into a bar chart and share your findings with a classmate.

Y=Yes and N=No

1. Do you google to find out information?

    Y N   Y N   Y N   Y N   Y N   Y N   Y N   Y N   Y N   Y N

2. Do you have your own webpage?

    Y N   Y N   Y N   Y N   Y N   Y N   Y N   Y N   Y N   Y N

3. Have you travelled by plane outside of Ireland?

    Y N   Y N   Y N   Y N   Y N   Y N   Y N   Y N   Y N   Y N

4. Have you downloaded music or movies from the internet?

    Y N   Y N   Y N   Y N   Y N   Y N   Y N   Y N   Y N   Y N

5. Do you watch satellite TV?

    Y N   Y N   Y N   Y N   Y N   Y N   Y N   Y N   Y N   Y N

6. Do you communicate with family/friends through Facebook?

    Y N   Y N   Y N   Y N   Y N   Y N   Y N   Y N   Y N   Y N

7. Do you use email?

    Y N   Y N   Y N   Y N   Y N   Y N   Y N   Y N   Y N   Y N

8. Do you buy goods (books, clothes, etc.) over the internet?

    Y N   Y N   Y N   Y N   Y N   Y N   Y N   Y N   Y N   Y N

9. Do you organise tickets (travel, cinema, theatre) over the internet?

    Y N   Y N   Y N   Y N   Y N   Y N   Y N   Y N   Y N   Y N

10. Do you buy things online from places outside of Ireland?

    Y N   Y N   Y N   Y N   Y N   Y N   Y N   Y N   Y N   Y N

In the table below put in a tick (✔) under the age heading for each person you survey.

	Under 13	13–19 years	20–40 years	41–59 years	Over 60
Age of Person					

Strand 02 Review

In this strand, you learned about:

- Development in an ever-changing world ☐
- Local development ☐
- Development and planning ☐
- Sustainable development and the SDGs ☐
- Poverty at home and abroad ☐
- Overcoming poverty: charity, solidarity, justice ☐

- Globalisation: our small world ☐
- The developing world ☐
- Trade: bananas, coffee ☐
- A campaign for sustainability: Fairtrade ☐
- Technology and sustainable development ☐
- And you carried out an action ☐

Look back over the lessons and activities that you have completed.
In the table below, tick the skills that you may have used or learned.

Managing myself	Staying well	Managing information and thinking	Being numerate
I know myself better ☐	I am healthy and active ☐	I was curious ☐	I expressed ideas mathematically ☐
I made decisions ☐	I am social ☐	I gathered and analysed information ☐	I estimated, predicted and calculated ☐
I set goals ☐	I am safe ☐	I thought creatively ☐	I was interested in problem-solving ☐
I achieved goals ☐	I feel confident ☐	I thought about what I learned ☐	I saw patterns and trends ☐
I thought about what I learned ☐	I feel positive about what I learned ☐	I used digital technology to access, manage and share information ☐	I gathered and presented data using digital technology to review and understand numbers ☐
I used technology to learn ☐			

Being creative	Working with others	Communicating	Being literate
I used my imagination ☐	I developed relationships ☐	I used language ☐	I understand some new words ☐
I thought about things from a different point of view ☐	I dealt with conflict ☐	I used numbers ☐	I enjoyed words and language ☐
I put ideas into action ☐	I co-operated ☐	I listened to my classmates ☐	I wrote for different reasons ☐
I learned in a creative way ☐	I respected difference ☐	I expressed myself ☐	I expressed my ideas clearly ☐
I was creative with digital technology ☐	I helped make the world a better place ☐	I performed/ presented ☐	I developed my spoken language ☐
	I learned with others ☐	I had a discussion/ debate ☐	I read and wrote in different ways ☐
	I worked with others using digital technology ☐	I used technology to communicate ☐	

Now write down two skills from the list that you think you should focus on more in the future.

_____

Power and decision-making

Overview of power and decision-making

Abraham Lincoln, when he was US President, described democracy as 'government of the people, for the people, by the people'. When studying power and decision-making you learn about how Ireland is governed, how we are part of intergovernmental organisations: the Council of Europe, the European Union and the United Nations.

You learn about important people in Ireland who hold positions of power: Uachtarán an hÉireann (President of Ireland), An Taoiseach, An Tánaiste, Ministers, TDs and Senators. You find out about how laws come into being and discover how our democratic government works.

One of the powers you have as a citizen is the power to vote. This right was won for you in the past, so when you are 18 years old, you will be responsible for casting your vote. So, you will know what to do when it comes to voting in an election or a referendum.

You may not be able to vote yet, but you are still a citizen and you can make your voice heard. You can contact your local TDs, your MEPs and your local councillors. You can get involved in campaigns and signing petitions.

You may already be involved in your Student Council, in Comhairle na nÓg or perhaps Dáil na nÓg! These are interesting ways in which to experience democracy in action.

Ireland plays an important role in the global community through our involvement in the Council of Europe, the European Union and the United Nations.

How politics affects me

Think about how politics and government influences your daily, weekly and monthly life. How does politics and government affect where you live, your music and your sport? Use the speech bubbles to share your answers.

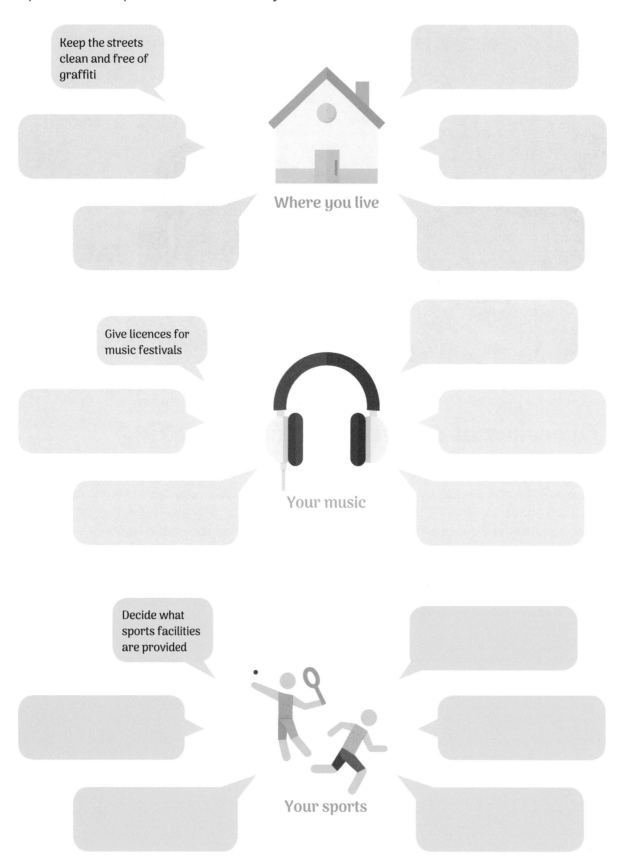

Culture box for Ireland today

Different people have dfferent cultures. Use this page to name or draw items you would put in your culture box for Ireland today. Share with a classmate.

Uachtarán na hÉireann (President of Ireland)

Place a photograph of the President of Ireland here.

Fill in the details about the current President of Ireland.

Name: _____

Date of birth: _____

Date elected President: _____

Term of office: _____

Name **two** priority areas that the President of Ireland is working on.

1. _____

2. _____

List **two** interesting facts about the President of Ireland.

1. _____

2. _____

Now write an email to the President asking to visit Aras an Uachtaráin. Give **three** reasons why you and your CSPE class would like to visit.

Write down **two** questions that you would like to ask the President on your visit.

_____

_____

Who needs a government?

We have a government for many reasons: to make laws, to collect taxes, to ensure that Ireland's interests are protected, to develop the country, to have a voice in international affairs and so on.

Below is a list of 10 reasons why we have a government. Your task is to rank each reason, with 1 being the most important reason for having a government in your opinion, and 10 being the least important reason. Explain your choice.

Rank	Reason	Explanation
	To provide information for people	
	To keep the economy safe	
	To look after the welfare of citizens	
	To have a strong army	
	To protect religious freedom	
	To collect taxes	
	To pass good and fair laws	
	To protect people's rights	
	To protect Ireland's natural resources	
	To have a voice on the international stage	

Match the job title with the work that the person holding this office does below.

1	Taoiseach	A	Chairs the sessions of the Dáil and keeps order there
2	Party Whip	B	Stands in for the Taoiseach when he or she is absent
3	Tánaiste	C	Ensures that all people in the political party know which way to vote
4	Ceann Comhairle	D	Is elected to represent people in her or his constituency
5	TD	E	Is the leader of the government

1 _____, 2 _____, 3 _____, 4 _____, 5 _____

Who am I?

A Minister is a TD who has been selected by the Taoiseach to lead a particular department in the government. I am a Minister. This means I have two roles to play. I have to look after the people in the area where I am elected and I have to work in the government department where I am the Minister. I hold a regular clinic in my constituency, where I meet the local people and look after their problems and concerns.

If the Dáil is sitting, then I have to be in the Dáil Chamber in Leinster House. It is important that I am there to answer parliamentary questions (PQs) on education, to help agree the order of business, to debate and discuss issues and to vote with the government. I also have to attend the Seanad when it is discussing laws relating to education.

I spend as much time as I can in my department. I go there before and after the Dáil sits some days, and on days when the Dáil is not sitting. Sometimes, I am asked to speak at events like the launch of a book or report, to open a new school or university, to visit a class or to see a display of students' work. Sometimes in March, I am invited to represent Ireland at the St Patrick's Day parade in another part of the world. I am often asked to go on radio or television to answer questions or to explain policies on education. I sometimes call press conferences with the media to announce plans and to answer questions. In the evening I am invited to meetings and social events, so sometimes my day is very long.

Who am I? _____

What is my name? _____

What is the full title of the department that I am in charge of?

_____

What party am I a member of? _____

What constituency do I represent? _____

The leader of this political party is: _____

What question would you ask this Minister if he or she knocked on your door at election time? Why? _____

_____

_____

Who is behind the door?

Bunreacht na hÉireann states that there can only be 15 Ministers as part of the Cabinet. Sometimes there may be more than 15 government departments! On the nameplates below fill in the Minister's department and his or her name.

An Taoiseach
_____

An Tánaiste
_____

_____

_____
_____

_____
_____

_____
_____

_____
_____

_____
_____

_____
_____

_____
_____

_____
_____

_____
_____

_____
_____

_____
_____

_____
_____

The language of politics

Terms: election time   candidate   polling card   **ballot paper**
TD   **general election**   referendum   PR

1. Use the terms above to fill in the blank spaces below.

    Caitríona was on her way to the polling station because it was
    _____ _____. There had not been a _____ _____
    for five years and Caitríona had been too young to vote then. But she had voted
    before. Just after her eighteenth birthday, there had been a _____ because
    the government had wanted to change the Constitution. That time she had voted
    YES. This time it would be different. She knew the _____ _____ would
    have many names on it and she would put the number 1 beside the name of
    the _____ she wanted to be elected. Then she would number all the other
    candidates. She remembered that in school they had been told this system of voting
    was called _____ _____. She had her _____ _____ in her
    pocket. It had come in the post last week and she would hand it in when she arrived
    at the polling station. She hoped that her candidate would be elected and become
    a _____ _____. It was about time there were more young people in the Dáil. Caitríona
    guessed it would take her only five minutes to vote. Then she would meet her mates.
    They were planning to see that new blockbuster movie!

2. Match the name of the Irish political party with the correct logo below, then make a copy
    of them in your own copy.

    Solidarity/PBP   Fianna Fáil   Fine Gael   **The Green Party**
    Labour Party   Sinn Féin   Social Democrats

For the want of a …

For the want of a VOTE
A QUOTA was lost
For the want of a QUOTA
A SEAT was lost
For the want of a SEAT
A MAJORITY was lost
For the want of a MAJORITY
A PARTY was lost
For the want of a PARTY
A GOVERNMENT was lost
And all for the want of a VOTE.

1. What is the message of this poem?

_____

_____

2. Why is it important to vote?

_____

_____

3. Explain each of the words in capital letters in the poem above.

VOTE _____

QUOTA _____

SEAT _____

MAJORITY _____

PARTY _____

GOVERNMENT _____

4. There is a suggestion that the voting age should be dropped to 16. Give **two** reasons why this is a good idea and create a slogan in support of this suggestion.

Reason 1:

Reason 2:

Slogan:

Election count analysis

Working out the quota in an election

The quota is calculated as follows:

$$\frac{\text{Number of valid votes}}{\text{Number of seats} + 1} + 1$$

For this by-election, there is one available seat. And the total valid poll is
(total poll − spoiled votes: 30,813 − 237) = 30,576

$$\frac{30,567}{1 + 1} + 1 = \mathbf{15,289}$$

	Election	By-election
Number of seats		1
Electorate		46,405
Total poll		30,813
Turnout		66.4%
Spoiled votes		237
Total valid poll		30,576
Quota		15,289

Candidate	1st count	2nd count	3rd count	
Henry, Oran (IND)	9, 419	9,419 + 1,750 = 11,169	11,169 + 2,813 = 13,982	Elected without reaching the quota
Murray, Richard (FG)	8,184	8,184 + 2,534 = 10,718	10,718 + 2,713 = 13,431	
McArdle, Lorcan (FF)	6,959	6,959 + 1,097 = 8,056	Eliminated	
Lyons, Brid (LAB)	5,133	Eliminated		
McNulty, Sarah (SF)	784	Eliminated		
Burke, Jarlath (GP)	97	Eliminated		
Total number of votes	30,576	30,576	30,576	
Non-transferable votes		633	2,530	
6 candidates				

Analyse the information from the election count above, and answer the following questions.

(a) What is a by-election?

(b) What was the quota for this by-election?

(c) How many people voted in this election?

(d) Who was eliminated after the first count?

(e) Which political party does Brid Lyons represent?

(f) Who won the by-election?

(g) Many young people do not cast their votes. Why do some young people not vote?

(h) Suggest **two** ways young people could be encouraged to vote.

The power jigsaw

Use the jigsaw pieces below to show which powers are those of the national government and which powers are of local government.

Use green to colour in jigsaw pieces that represent national government powers.
Use red to colour in jigsaw pieces that represent local government powers.

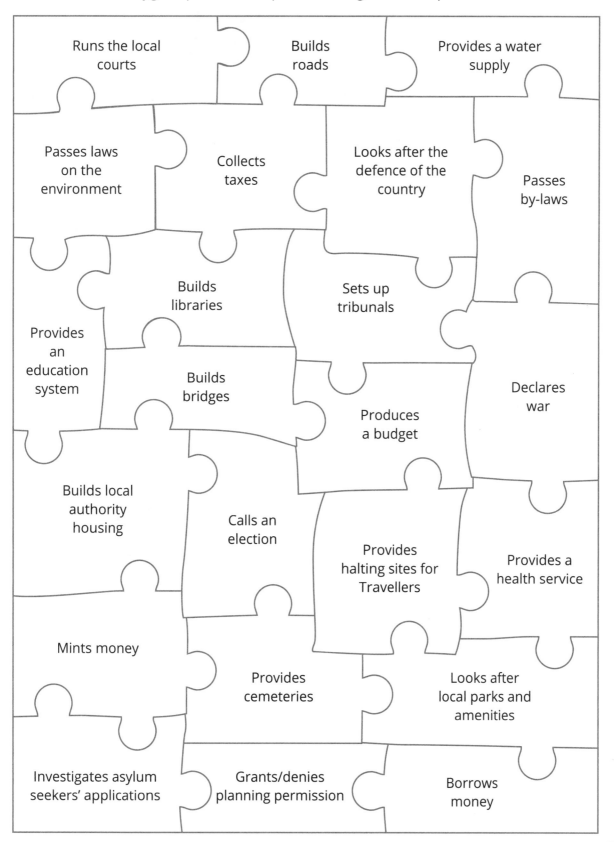

Vote for me for the Student Council!

These students have decided to run for the Student Council as representatives for their class. Read their campaign speeches and decide which one you would vote for.

Tick the candidate you would vote for, then give reasons for your choice.

I am on the school Gaelic and soccer teams and I swim every day, rain or shine. I think we need to improve all the sports facilities in the school and if I'm elected, I will fight hard for this goal.

Lorcan ☐

My big campaign issue is bullying. I know we don't have much bullying in this school and I want to keep it that way. I would like to set up an anti-bullying committee and have an anti-bullying week.

Eoghan ☐

I have won many drama prizes and I have won medals for making speeches. I will be the best person to represent the views of the class and at speaking out for your issues.

Martin ☐

Úna ☐

Everybody says I'm a very good listener and I will be good at listening to what the class wants. I believe in fairness and will fight hard for this. Fair treatment for all is the big issue.

My opinion is that it is important that girls have equal opportunities on sports teams and other clubs in the school. I will make sure that girls get a fair share.

☐ Larissa

I think that clubs after school is a big problem in this school. I will fight to have more clubs where we can do art, cookery, chess and computers. There's nothing to do here after school and I want to change that.

Dorota ☐

Reasons for my choice:

_____

_____

_____

_____

_____

Themus Island conflict

In a faraway corner of the world there is an island called Themus. There are two tribes of people; the Thems believe that mountains are more important than the sea and another, the Usses, believe that the sea is more important than mountains.

Whenever these two groups meet, there is trouble. They argue and fight over the sea and the mountains. These troubles have gone on for generations. At times, there has been violence between the two groups. Because of all the trouble, the two groups now live at opposite ends of the island. The adult Thems and Usses never spend time with each other. The only time the two sides meet is when they drop off their children at the one school on the island.

Everybody on Themus is fed up with all the trouble and wants it to end. A special committee has been set up to offer some suggestions to the Thems and the Usses.

Look at the suggestions below and rank the 10 suggested solutions in order from 1 to 10: 1 is the best solution and 10 is the worst. Explain your ranking in your copy.

Build a second school and keep the two sides completely separate.		Bring in the army and force one side to agree with the other.	
Put the Usses in prison if they say that the sea is better than mountains. Put the Thems in prison if they say that mountains are better than the sea.		Encourage the Thems and the Usses to respect the fact that not everyone believes the same thing. They could start learning this at school.	
Bring the two sides together to see if they can agree on some things and begin again from there.		Arm the two sides so that they can have a proper war and finally end the troubles.	
Banish all the Usses to another island.		Banish all the Thems to another island.	
Get the Thems and the Usses to argue more so that they get fed up and stop.		Build a big wall and divide the island in two.	

Can you think of other solutions?

_____

_____

Can you think of any real conflicts that are like the one on Themus?

Describe one of these conflicts.

_____

_____

_____

The EU stamps

Design a set of stamps to inform others about the seven EU Member States that you are least familiar with. Choose a landmark, famous person or a symbol closely associated with each of the seven countries.

Know your Europe

Fill in the details about the current EU Commissioner nominated by Ireland.

Place a photograph of the EU Commissioner here.

Name: _____

Date appointed EU Commissioner: _____

Term of office: _____

Commission area of responsibility: _____

1. Name **three** priority areas being worked on by this Commissioner.

   (a) _____

   (b) _____

   (c) _____

2. List **two** interesting facts about this EU Commissioner.

   (a) _____

   (b) _____

3. Here are **three** photographs of European Institutions. Match the name of the building with each picture.

Names: A. The European Central Bank; B. The European Court of Human Rights;
C. The European Parliament in Strasbourg

1 _____   **2** _____   **3** _____

The United Nations

Fill in the details about the current Secretary-General of the UN.

Name: _____

Date appointed UN Secretary-General: _____

Term of office: _____

Country of origin: _____

Place a photograph of the United Nations Secretary-General here.

1. Name **two** priority areas being worked on by the UN Secretary-General.

    (a) _____

    (b) _____

2. List **two** interesting facts about the UN Secretary-General.

    (a) _____

    (b) _____

3. Look closely at the image below and then answer the questions.

    (a) What is this image saying?

    _____

    _____

    (b) What does the dove represent? _____

    (c) Name **two** countries where Irish soldiers have served with the United Nations.

    Country (i) _____   Country (ii) _____

4. Suggest **one** activity your CSPE class could organise to mark United Nations Day (24 October) to raise awareness about the work of the United Nations.

    Activity: _____

Answers questioned

Write a question to match each of the answers below.

Q1 _____
Answer: The Constitution

Q2 _____
Answer: The UN Security Council

Q3 _____
Answer: Proportional Representation (PR)

Q4 _____
Answer: The European Commission

Q5 _____
Answer: The Houses of the Oireachtas

Q6 _____
Answer: Amhrán an bhFiann

Q7 _____
Answer: MEP

Q8 _____
Answer: An Tánaiste

Q9 _____
Answer: Referendum

Q10 _____
Answer: Teachta Dála (TD)

Q11 _____
Answer: The Council of Europe

Q12 _____
Answer: Uachtarán na hÉireann

Q13 _____
Answer: Strasbourg

Q14 _____
Answer: Constituency

Q15 _____
Answer: Northern Ireland Assembly

Q16 _____
Answer: Local authority

Q17 _____
Answer: Democracy

Q18 _____
Answer: 18 years of age

Q19 _____
Answer: The Harp

Q20 _____
Answer: Polling Station

09 The law and the citizen

Overview of the law and the citizen

Where would we be without laws? Laws are a very important part of our society. They help to keep order in the country, to protect life and property, and to guide people's behaviour. Laws are not a new invention – they have been with us in some form for centuries. Laws have the power to shape our society and to bring about change.

In Ireland, the government passes laws after a very careful process, which you learned about, in the last chapter. Laws are carried out by our police force, an Garda Síochána. We have a system of courts that deal with civil and criminal cases. There are prisons in different parts of the country, where criminals serve time for their crimes if convicted and sentenced to prison. People are also fined; receive suspended sentences, community service orders and penalty points as punishment for breaking the law.

The law affects all parts of our lives. For example, labour laws deal with working hours, and consumer laws deal with our rights as shoppers. We have laws that protect our environment, and traffic laws that deal with traffic offences such as speeding. The laws we have make our world a safer place.

Can you spot the crime at the crime scene?

1. How many crimes can you find in this picture? List them all in your copy.

2. Who are the victims of crime here?

_____

_____

_____

_____

_____

Criminal offences and offenders

1. Make a list of crimes under each of the following headings.

Minor offences	Serious offences	Extremely serious offences

2. If you were a judge, what punishment would you consider suitable for the following crimes?

(a) Joyriding – a second offence

_____

_____

_____

(b) Mugging – a third offence

_____

_____

_____

(c) House-breaking – a first offence

_____

_____

_____

(d) Vandalising a bus shelter – a second offence

_____

_____

_____

(e) Under-age drinking – a first offence

_____

_____

_____

Name the crime

Name the crimes that are being described in the sentences below.

Deliberately killing someone with intention is called _____

Killing someone, but without intention is called _____

Bringing goods across a country's border without paying the tax is called _____

Stealing from a person's home is called _____

Stealing from a person's bag is called _____

Forcing an airplane to go somewhere or land somewhere is called _____

A person who attacks another person in the street to rob them is called _____

Deliberately setting fire to something in a criminal way is called _____

Stealing something from a shop is called _____

Using information about a person to get money from them is called _____

Taking something out of a person's pocket is called _____

Making copies of bank notes is called _____

Spray painting walls or wrecking bus shelters is called _____

When a person is taken hostage in order to be paid for by ransom, this is called _____

When a person is forced to have sex against their will this is called _____

Paying officials money in order to get them to do something illegal is called _____

Being married to more than one person at the same time is called _____

Smashing windows and grabbing goods during protests is called _____

Selling a country's secret information to another country is called _____

Deceiving people for financial gain is called _____

Driving at 100 km/h in an 80 km/h zone is called _____

Taking funds belonging to your employer is called _____

It is the law: true or false?

Read each of the following statements and decide if they are true or false by circling the appropriate letter, then fill in the empty boxes with your own true/false statements about the law.

Hint: See Chapter 9 of your *Make a Difference!* textbook for ideas.

The highest court in Ireland is the High Court. T F	The largest award or claim in the District Court is €15,000. T F	All family law cases are held *in camera*, which means that they are not open to the public. T F
There are two prisons in Mountjoy, one for men and one for women. T F	There is always a jury in the Central Criminal Court. T F	It is the duty of the court to pass laws. T F
Women cannot become Supreme Court Judges. T F	The Supreme Court sits in the High Court in Dublin. T F	T F
T F	T F	T F
T F	T F	T F

People and courts

1. Match the job title below with the type of work each person does in relation to the law. You can use each name and issue only once.

1.	Barrister	a.	Arrests criminals
2.	Garda	b.	Keeps a written record of what people say in court
3.	Stenographer	c.	Is in charge of a prison
4.	Judge	d.	Studies the law to help people to make a good case
5.	Prison warden	e.	Makes decisions after hearing all the evidence

2. Fill in the gaps in the sentences below. The first letter in each word has been given to you.

   (a) The court that decides on matters that relate to the Constitution is called the

   S _____ C_____.

   (b) F_____ L_____ cases are heard *in camera*.

   (c) If you cannot afford a solicitor or barrister then you can get
   F_____ L_____ A_____.

   (d) The Minister for J_____ is in charge of the courts.

   (e) There are usually t_____ people on a jury.

   (f) H_____ are put on the wrists of criminals when bringing them to and from court.

   (g) You have to be e_____ years of age to sit on a jury.

   (h) When someone is found guilty of a crime, the judge hands a s_____ down to them.

3. Tick the one correct answer below.

The court that travels around the country is called:	In the Small Claims Court, the largest claim you can make is:
☐ **A** The Travelling Court	☐ **A** €500
☐ **B** The Circuit Court	☐ **B** €2,000
☐ **C** The District court	☐ **C** €3,000
The most judges you can have in the Supreme Court is:	If you sue someone for damaging your property this is a:
☐ **A** 3	☐ **A** Criminal case
☐ **B** 5	☐ **B** Civil case
☐ **C** 10	☐ **C** Basket case

Witness reports

The Sligo bus was involved in a crash. The Garda who arrived at the scene asked six witnesses what they had seen. They all made statements, but only one of them was correct – all the others made at least one mistake.

1. Read the following witness statements and decide which one is correct. Name one error that you can find in each of the incorrect statements.

    Witness A

    I was standing at the corner at about 10:00. I heard a loud bang. The Longford bus ran right into the bread van. The driver of the van shot out through the passenger door onto the road. He clearly wasn't wearing a seat belt. He was unconscious when I saw him.

    Witness B

    As I saw it, the bread van just pulled out right in front of the bus. The bus driver didn't stand a chance. I'm not too sure, but I think it happened at about 11:00. I get a bit confused sometimes.

    Witness C

    This is the fourth accident to happen at this spot in the last month. These young women bus drivers are dangerous. She took off at a great speed and just ploughed into the milk van. These women all drive too fast and aren't careful. They should sack the lot of them.

    Witness D

    I was on my way to the supermarket when it happened. I heard the sound of breaking glass and I thought it was some sort of bank raid. I ran around the corner to see what was happening. The bus had run straight into the front of the van. It was horrible.

    Witness E

    I could see that the driver of the bread van was hurt. I had my mobile phone with me, so I called the Gardaí. I was on my way to the dentist. I had a 10:00 appointment and I have missed it now. I'd say that the accident happened at about a quarter to ten. I hope he's going to be okay.

    Witness F

    I was just walking on the path across the road when it happened. The bread van was coming out of a side street, having delivered some bread to the deli. It looked to me like she didn't see the bus. There was a screech of brakes as the bus driver tried to stop. Luckily, no one was hurt.

2. In your copy write a short script looking for more witnesses of the crash for the TV programme *CrimeCall.*

    OR

    Imagine you have witnessed a shopkeeper being robbed of all her money. Write an account of the statement you might make to the Gardaí in your copy.

The Crime Victims Helpline

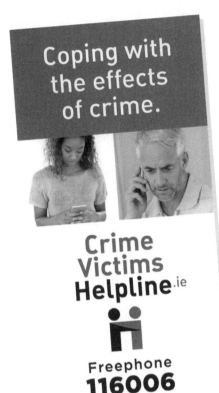

Coping with the effects of crime.

Crime Victims Helpline.ie

Freephone 116006

Text 085 1337711
info@crimevictimshelpline.ie
www.crimevictimshelpline.ie

Effects of Crime
If you are a victim of crime, you may feel:
- Alone or isolated
- Anxious or depressed
- Angry and let down

How do we help?
We are here to listen.
Our primary focus is on emotional support, providing the opportunity for you to talk about your experience in confidence.
We just listen with empathy, and without judgement.
If you feel isolated or do not know who to talk to, we are here to listen and to give you our time.
We can also help in liaising with the Gardaí and other agencies and services.

a service provided by the Commission of Victims of Crime and provided by volunteers.

We provide information on
- Local support services where available
- Services available for victims of particular crimes
- All aspects of the criminal justice system
- Rights and entitlements regarding compensation, legal aid, the courts

www.crimevictimshelpline.ie
info@crimevictimshelpline.ie

Read the brochure above and answer the questions below in your copy.

1. Name **three** effects of crime.

   (a) _____

   (b) _____

   (c) _____

2. What is the email address of the organisation that produced this leaflet?

   _____

3. Who does the leaflet say you can contact if you need to talk to someone?

   _____

4. List **three** things that this organisation provides.

   (a) _____

   (b) _____

   (c) _____

5. Do you think that the victims of crime need support? Explain your answer.

   _____

   _____

6. There is no slogan on this leaflet. Compose a suitable slogan for this organisation.

   _____

Caught red-handed!

A shopkeeper was concerned that
money was going missing from the
tills and so installed a secret security
camera. A few days later, a shop
assistant was caught on camera
putting money in his pocket. When
the assistant was about to leave for
home that evening the shop manager
called him in to the office and played
the recording.

1. Describe **two** possible consequences for this person now.

_____

_____

_____

_____

_____

_____

_____

_____

_____

_____

Share these with others in your class to cover all the possible consequences.

2. Describe **two** possible consequences for this person in the future.

_____

_____

_____

_____

_____

_____

_____

_____

Share these with others in your class to cover all the possible consequences.

Ballygosloe

Ballygosloe is a small town in Ireland, not too far from you. It has a terrible problem as many cars are speeding around the place. The speed limit is 50 km/h in the town and 80 km/h on the roads outside the town. Nearly everyone seems to ignore the speed limit.

The people who were caught speeding made excuses like:

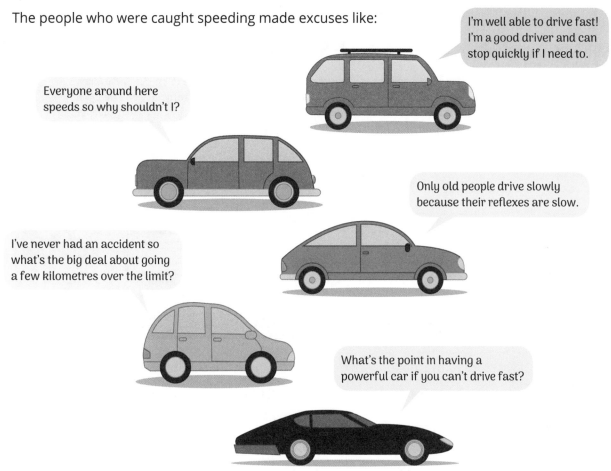

I'm well able to drive fast! I'm a good driver and can stop quickly if I need to.

Everyone around here speeds so why shouldn't I?

Only old people drive slowly because their reflexes are slow.

I've never had an accident so what's the big deal about going a few kilometres over the limit?

What's the point in having a powerful car if you can't drive fast?

The number of crashes that have happened in Ballygosloe worries the Road Safety Authority. They want to send a car sticker into every home, this will go on the back of cars to remind people to slow down. Your task is to design the car sticker.

Ballygosloe

The Garda Reserve

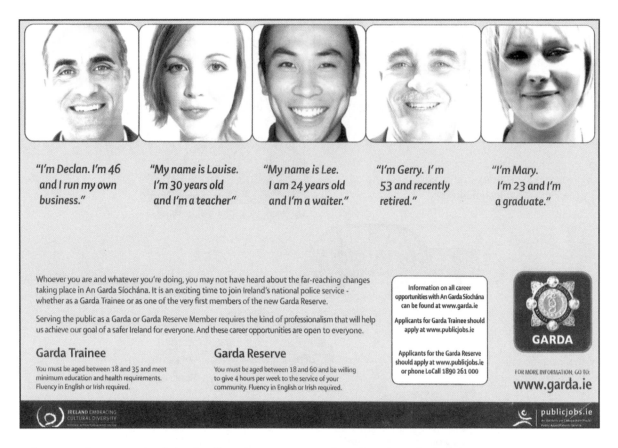

"I'm Declan. I'm 46 and I run my own business."

"My name is Louise. I'm 30 years old and I'm a teacher"

"My name is Lee. I am 24 years old and I'm a waiter."

"I'm Gerry. I'm 53 and recently retired."

"I'm Mary. I'm 23 and I'm a graduate."

Whoever you are and whatever you're doing, you may not have heard about the far-reaching changes taking place in An Garda Síochána. It is an exciting time to join Ireland's national police service - whether as a Garda Trainee or as one of the very first members of the new Garda Reserve.

Serving the public as a Garda or Garda Reserve Member requires the kind of professionalism that will help us achieve our goal of a safer Ireland for everyone. And these career opportunities are open to everyone.

Garda Trainee

You must be aged between 18 and 35 and meet minimum education and health requirements. Fluency in English or Irish required.

Garda Reserve

You must be aged between 18 and 60 and be willing to give 4 hours per week to the service of your community. Fluency in English or Irish required.

Information on all career opportunities with An Garda Síochána can be found at www.garda.ie

Applicants for Garda Trainee should apply at www.publicjobs.ie

Applicants for the Garda Reserve should apply at www.publicjobs.ie or phone LoCall 1890 261 000

GARDA

FOR MORE INFORMATION, GO TO:
www.garda.ie

IRELAND EMBRACING CULTURAL DIVERSITY

publicjobs.ie

When you have studied the leaflet above answer the questions below in your copy.

1. According to the advertisement, what is the goal of the Garda and the Garda Reserve?

   _____

2. (a) What age must you be to become a trainee Garda?

   _____

   (b) What age must you be to become a member of the Garda Reserve?

   _____

   (c) How much time must you be willing to give in the service of your community to become a member of the Garda Reserve?

   _____

3. (a) Why do you think people must be fluent in Irish or English to join these forces?

   _____

   _____

   (b) Where does the advertisement say you can get more information on these forces?

   _____

3. Name **two** actions that the Minister for Justice could take to encourage more people to join the Garda Reserve.

   (a) _____

   (b) _____

Crime and punishment

Imagine it is 2070 and the law has changed in order to keep crime at a minimum. Now petty criminals wear a collar with a tiny tracking device so that the Gardaí always know where they are. Other criminals are branded on the forehead and people wearing a brand are not allowed into certain places or to hold certain jobs.

More criminals are deported and sent off to a space station, where they don't meet other people until their sentence is served.

Finally, dangerous criminals are given brain transplants from good-living people who have died in traffic accidents.

1. What are the advantages and disadvantages of the four methods described above?

_____

_____

_____

_____

2. Which of the **four** methods do you like best? Why?

_____

_____

_____

3. Which of the **four** methods do you think is unlikely to ever happen?

_____

_____

_____

4. Describe another suitable punishment that could be used in the future.

_____

_____

The real victim

Read the following story and answer the questions that follow.

A 70-year-old woman lost the last photographs of her late husband and her wedding ring when a burglar broke into her home and took her handbag. Yvonne Daly, who is disabled, had been asleep in the sheltered housing complex on the outskirts of Dunskeagh, when a young teenager, who cannot be named for legal reasons, broke in through the bathroom window in the middle of the night on the 24 February.

The 16-year-old teenager fled after grabbing Mrs Daly's handbag. He stole €22, but dumped her bag with the precious photographs and the ring. These have never been found. Mrs Daly raised the alarm herself when she woke the following morning and found that her handbag was no longer beside the bed. She later discovered broken glass in the bathroom.

The Gardaí were called, took statements and dusted for fingerprints. They were able to identify the culprit and an arrest followed.

After hearing the case, the judge sentenced the teenager to 12 months in a young offender's prison outside the city.

The judge said it must have been a very frightening experience for Mrs Daly to know that someone had broken into her home, and to have actually been in her bedroom as she slept. The judge told the teenager that he had committed, 'a very nasty crime'. 'It is not about the money' the judge said, 'but about the loss of the photographs and the ring that can never be replaced'. The teenager, it was revealed, has previous convictions for theft and handling stolen goods.

The teenager, who had free legal aid, asked his solicitor to tell the court that he was 'ashamed' of what he had done and was genuinely sorry for the woman's loss. The solicitor explained that the teenager had been out of control for a while following the death of a brother in a tragic car accident the previous year. The teenager's mother was in tears following the sentencing.

1. Why was this a particularly nasty crime?

   _____

   _____

   _____

2. Was the punishment given to the teenager here fair? Explain your answer.

   _____

   _____

   _____

4. Does the fact that the teenager was out of control for a while excuse the behaviour? Explain your answer.

   _____

   _____

   _____

5. Imagine you are Mrs Daly and you are given the chance to make a victim impact statement where you can explain how the teenager's crime has affected you. Write out the statement in your copy.

Emergency calls

In each of the following cases, 1, 2, 3, 4 and 5, complete the emergency call.

1. You see someone has been knocked off his or her bike and is unconscious.
2. You see someone has fallen into a river.
3. You see someone is trying to break into your neighbour's house.
4. You see flames coming out of a house.
5. You see someone who says they have lost their cat!

What number do you dial? Which service do you need?

1. _____
2. _____
3. _____
4. _____
5. _____

What is your name? Where are you?

1. Jay Bloggs _____
2. Jay Bloggs _____
3. Jay Bloggs _____
4. Jay Bloggs _____
5. Jay Bloggs _____

Tell me slowly what has happened?

1. _____
   _____
   _____

2. _____
   _____
   _____

3. _____
   _____
   _____

4. _____
   _____
   _____

5. _____
   _____
   _____

The crime of shoplifting

Look at the poster and read the passage, then answer the questions below in your copy.

A small shopkeeper who has been part of the local community for many years is about to close down his shop because shoplifting is costing him €10,000 a year. Even though the owner of The Gem store, Mr Flynn, spent €2,000 on a CCTV camera and a 24-hour alarm system, it has not stopped the thieves from robbing him. He even got a security company to drive by at night to try to stop people from attempting to rob-and-run before the alarm alerted the Gardaí.

He said that it is very expensive to prosecute shoplifters in court, which he always does if someone is caught and the shoplifters rarely get prison sentences.

Mr Flynn said, 'Shoplifting is a huge problem these days. People think it is a soft crime because no one gets hurt, but I'm getting hurt … I think that the shoplifters are looking for money for drugs or have personal problems … then some kids do it for the thrill. But I've had enough, and am going to close my doors. I hate leaving the community high and dry but I can't survive anymore.'

WIN A FREE RIDE!

IN A GARDA CAR JUST BY SHOPLIFTING FROM THIS STORE.

Make Mam and Dad proud!

1. What steps did the owner of The Gem shop take, to try to stop the shoplifting?

2. What point is Mr Flynn making about prosecuting the thieves in court?

3. Why is shoplifting seen as a 'soft crime'?

4. According to the passage above, why do people commit the crime of shoplifting?

5. What other reasons can you think of to explain people committing this crime?

6. How does shoplifting affect shop owners?

7. How does the local community suffer because of the crime of shoplifting?

8. What is the message in the poster above?

9. How might parents feel if their son or daughter is caught shoplifting?

10. It has been suggested that when found guilty, shoplifters should be made to stand outside the store that they stole from wearing a sign that says, 'I am a thief. I stole from this store.' What do you think of this suggestion? Is there a human dignity issue here? What would be a suitable punishment for the crime of shoplifting?

11. Compose an anti-shoplifting slogan.

Law survey

Your class want to carry out a survey as a way of finding out information about people's attitudes. You have decided to investigate the law in Ireland.

(a) Name **three** areas of the law that you will focus on in the survey and explain why you have picked those areas.

_____

_____

_____

_____

(b) Write out **six** questions that you think would be important to include in your questionnaire and explain why you would ask **each** of them.

_____

_____

_____

_____

_____

_____

_____

_____

(c) Write a paragraph explaining what you would do with all the information that you collect.

_____

_____

_____

_____

_____

_____

_____

_____

_____

_____

The power of the law

At one time people travelled around Ireland on foot or by horse and cart. Laws had to be passed to regulate society as cars became more common. Fill in the wall below with the laws you think were needed to manage traffic, protect drivers and their passengers and pedestrians. Two have been done for you.

Cars that are 10 years old and over must pass an NCT test every year and cars from 4 to 9 years old must pass a test every 2 years.

ATTENTION / ACHTUNG

**Drive on left
Conduire à gauche
Links fahren**

In Ireland you must drive on the left-hand side of the road.

The role of the media

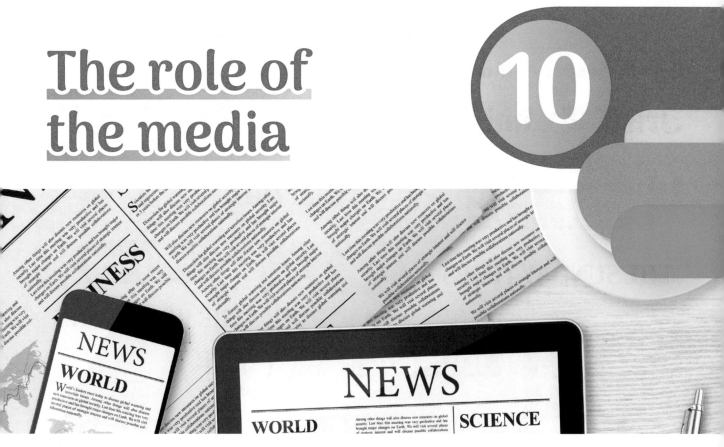

Overview of the role of the media

Today, information is easily accessible. TV, cable TV, radio, print and online newspapers, magazines, books, billboards, the internet, tablets and smart phones are all sources of information. These media platforms provide news, education, information and opinion whenever, and in some cases, wherever you want it.

People with camera phones have become citizen journalists. Eyewitnesses take photos on mobile phones and make video recordings of events; and sometimes it is the ordinary person who first breaks the story to the world.

Media platforms will select the stories they want to tell. Some stories are never covered. The editor will choose the story and decide on the viewpoint. This opinion influences the reader or viewer and tries to persuade people to think in the same way. Public opinion can be shaped like this.

The term 'new media' includes the interactive, screen-based, digital (computer) technology involving images, text and sound. This new digitised media content has developed over the past 20 years. It is all about the internet and computers, e-books, cable and satellite TV, mp3 and mp4 files, streamed music and movies.

'Social media' refers to a group of popular online and internet-based applications that are used for social interaction among large groups of people. By being aware of your cyber-surroundings and whom you are talking to online, you should be able to safely enjoy social networking.

It is said that 'knowledge is power'. For citizens living in a democracy, the giving and receiving of accurate information is important, as it means that informed choices can be made. Terms such as bias, spin, fake news and 'alternative facts' have become part of our vocabulary.

As we are bombarded with so much information, it is more important than ever to check the facts fully before believing them. Always double-check, or triple-check even, in order to find the truth!

Newspaper hunt

THE SUNDAY TIMES

THE IRISH TIMES

 Sunday Independent

Independent.ie

Name **four** daily newspapers in Ireland.

1. _____
2. _____
3. _____
4. _____

Name **four** Sunday newspapers in Ireland.

1. _____
2. _____
3. _____
4. _____

Name **four** online, digital newspapers in Ireland.

1. _____
2. _____
3. _____
4. _____

Name **three** newspapers that have both print and digital newspapers.

1. _____
2. _____
3. _____

Breaking news

Write down a possible breaking news story under each of the following headings, an idea has been suggested under each heading, but you can create your own if you prefer. Then read out your story like a TV news reporter – fast, clear and clipped.

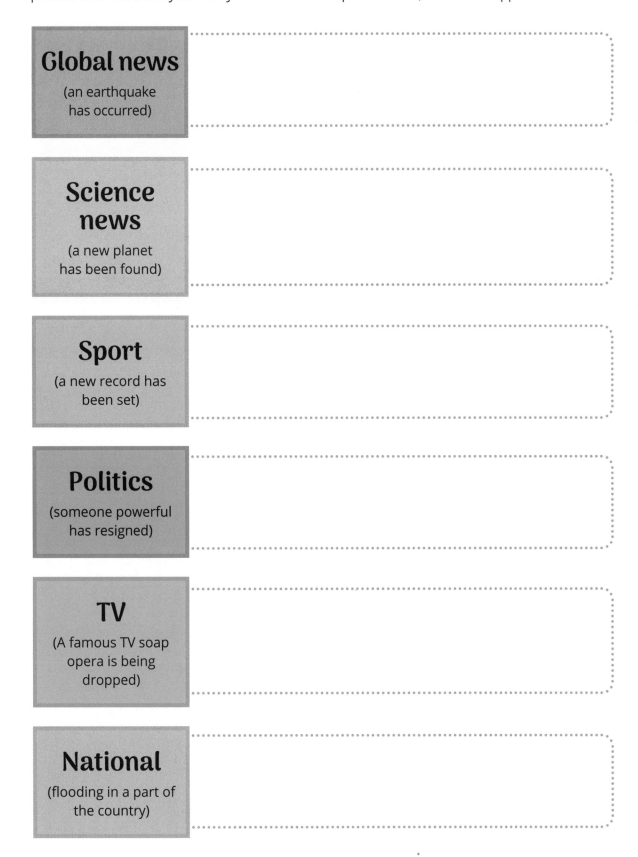

Global news
(an earthquake has occurred)

Science news
(a new planet has been found)

Sport
(a new record has been set)

Politics
(someone powerful has resigned)

TV
(A famous TV soap opera is being dropped)

National
(flooding in a part of the country)

Exploring media language

Look at the words below and sort them into the correct box. Some will go into more than one box.

email	documentary	sitcom	**fashion report**	party political broadcast
tabloid	**soap opera**	phone-in	broadsheet	current affairs programme
text message	sports report	**traffic update**	cartoon	weather report
interview	biography	advertisement	tweet	**letter to the editor**

Newspapers/Magazines	Radio	Television	Digital media

Use the words above to complete the following task:

Description	Word
A programme about important political or social events that are happening at the time.	
Short messages of 140 characters.	
A type of newspaper with a large format, regarded as more serious than tabloids.	
A report based on questions that people are asked about themselves.	
A funny show, usually on TV, where the same characters are facing different situations in every episode.	
A way of communicating on the internet that has replaced using letters in many cases.	
Booklets that tell a story using pictures and speech bubbles.	
People call a show and express their opinions or tell their own personal stories, then others comment on this.	
A programme or film about something factual.	
A politician speaks a message to the people.	

Choose any **five** of the types of media on this page and give an example of each. One has been done for you.

1. Phone-in: LIVELINE Joe Duffy

2. _____

3. _____

4. _____

5. _____

Social networking apps

Networking applications (Facebook, Twitter, Myspace, Instagram, Snapchat, etc.) are great places to catch up with friends and to meet new people. Sometimes, however, people give away too much information online. Your photos, video clips and blogs might be getting you noticed in ways that you do not want.

1. Your CSPE class has decided to raise awareness about wellbeing and safety for young people online. Write down **three** pieces of safety advice you would email to a friend who is planning to set up a profile on Facebook.

   _____
   _____
   _____
   _____

2. Design a bookmark, in the box provided, entitled 'Be Safe Online'. Create a logo and a number of bullet points highlighting the important 'Dos and Don'ts' of being online.

3. Describe **two** other actions that your CSPE class could take to raise awareness about the importance of safety online for students in your school.

   Action 1: _____
   _____
   _____
   _____

   Action 2: _____
   _____
   _____
   _____

Citizenship in the digital age

Study the infographic below and and create your own infographic here on being a responsible digital citizen in Ireland.

FOLENS
Wellbeing

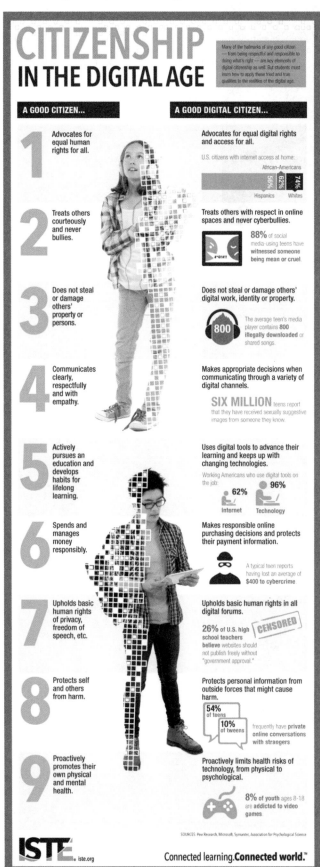

Cyberbullying

Jakub is under a lot of pressure from his parents to do well in school. Other students in school slag him because he tries so hard but still gets bad results in his exams. He gets instant messages and text messages during the day and at night. The word 'loser' appears in most of them. Jakub thinks he knows who is behind the messages. He thinks its Sorcha, the most popular girl in Third Year! To get back at Sorcha, Jakub sends her this message: 'I'm going to kill you for doing this. Your friends, too.'

FOLENS
Wellbeing

Ur just a loser!

1. How do you think Jakub feels? What is it about this situation that is making him feel this way?

    _____

    _____

    _____

2. What should Sorcha do?

    _____

    _____

    _____

3. What could Jakub have done instead of sending the message to Sorcha?

    _____

    _____

    _____

4. What should the other students, who knew Jakub was receiving these messages, have done?

    _____

    _____

    _____

Most students would have no problem reporting cyberbullying if they did not have to identify themselves. **Remember: Everyone has a right not to be bullied online or in person.**

5. Jot down as many ways as possible that you could anonymously report cyberbullying in your school.

    _____

    _____

    _____

    _____

    _____

Tweets

Write some tweets, a tweet has 140 characters.

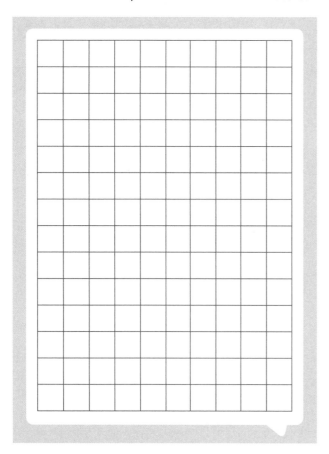

You are going to run for the office of President of Ireland. Write a tweet that you would send to get people to support you in the presidential election.

You as a citizen want to organise a protest march against some problem in society or in your local area. Write out the tweet that you would send to rally support for this event.

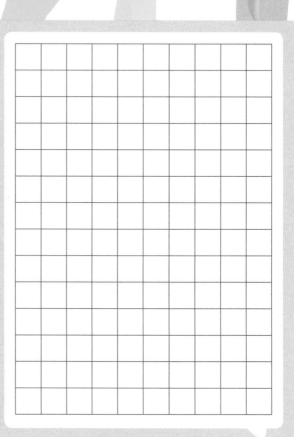

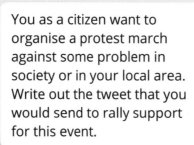

Making the news

Write a newspaper article about something happening in the world today using the template below as a guide.

Headlines
Catches the attention

Important information
Who? What? Where? When?

Tail – conclusion

Less important information and more details

Name of paper

Day	Date

Headline

Story outline

Suitable image

Story in detail

Confusing news

1. Examine this cartoon. Describe what is happening in the cartoon.

   _____
   _____
   _____
   _____
   _____
   _____

2. What does this cartoon tell us about the world we live in?

   _____
   _____
   _____
   _____
   _____
   _____

3. What does it tell us about video and online games?

   _____
   _____
   _____
   _____
   _____
   _____

Strand 03 Review

In this strand, you learned about:

- Democracy and the role of the citizen ☐
- Ireland and identity ☐
- The government of Ireland ☐
- Making laws, voting and elections ☐
- Northern Ireland and the peace process ☐
- Ireland and Europe ☐
- The United Nations ☐

- The Irish legal and prison systems ☐
- An Garda Síochána ☐
- Young people and the law in action ☐
- Power of the law to bring about change ☐
- The role of the media in a democracy ☐
- Social media, fake news and cyberbullying ☐
- And you carried out an action ☐

Look back over the lessons and activities that you have completed.
In the table below, tick the skills that you may have used or learned.

Managing myself	Staying well	Managing information and thinking	Being numerate
I know myself better ☐ I made decisions ☐ I set goals ☐ I achieved goals ☐ I thought about what I learned ☐ I used technology to learn ☐	I am healthy and active ☐ I am social ☐ I am safe ☐ I feel confident ☐ I feel positive about what I learned ☐	I was curious ☐ I gathered and analysed information ☐ I thought creatively ☐ I thought about what I learned ☐ I used digital technology to access, manage and share information ☐	I expressed ideas mathematically ☐ I estimated, predicted and calculated ☐ I was interested in problem-solving ☐ I saw patterns and trends ☐ I gathered and presented data using digital technology to review and understand numbers ☐

Being creative	Working with others	Communicating	Being literate
I used my imagination ☐ I thought about things from a different point of view ☐ I put ideas into action ☐ I learned in a creative way ☐ I was creative with digital technology ☐	I developed relationships ☐ I dealt with conflict ☐ I co-operated ☐ I respected difference ☐ I helped make the world a better place ☐ I learned with others ☐ I worked with others using digital technology ☐	I used language ☐ I used numbers ☐ I listened to my classmates ☐ I expressed myself ☐ I performed/presented ☐ I had a discussion/debate ☐ I used technology to communicate ☐	I understand some new words ☐ I enjoyed words and language ☐ I wrote for different reasons ☐ I expressed my ideas clearly ☐ I developed my spoken language ☐ I read and wrote in different ways ☐

Now write down two skills from the list that you think you should focus on more in the future.

_____

11 Action, reflection and assessment

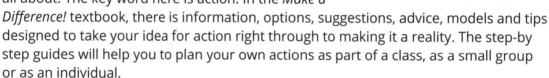

Overview of action, reflection and assessment

Using your power as a young citizen to take action is an important step in learning what being a citizen is all about. The key word here is action. In the *Make a Difference!* textbook, there is information, options, suggestions, advice, models and tips designed to take your idea for action right through to making it a reality. The step-by step guides will help you to plan your own actions as part of a class, as a small group or as an individual.

Sometimes, it can be useful to have worksheets to help you to plan and focus your action. We have included many useful tools here to help you to record important aspects of your actions. For example, a diary entry record, a page to help you manage and record meetings of your group, team or committee; to keep notes of strong feelings and thoughts that you have while doing your action; to record your progress; to evaluate the action when you have finished.

Sometimes, it is easy to let learning happen, to go through the motions and not to think too much about it. This chapter asks you to reflect. Reflection is about stopping to think, to ponder and to consider. You can do it to plan for action, you can do it while taking action, and you can do it about the action when it is finished. Reflecting this way – for, in and about action – will deepen your learning and help you to understand the world, and yourself, better.

Keeping a record of your work, your thoughts and your learning in CSPE over the three years is important too, but not a hard thing to do. For example, you could take photos, gather newspaper clippings, make videos and podcasts, collect leaflets and brochures about organisations or people in society. By shaping these with your own written work from this Student Activity Book and from your copy, you are making a portfolio that will capture your CSPE journey. Portfolios are not just for when you study art, they can become your own treasure chest of learning.

Since First Year, you have been exploring what it means to be a young citizen in Ireland and on the global stage. What sort of citizen will you be in the future? How interested will you be in the development of the world, in the environment? How active will you be in the interest of justice and human rights? How will you contribute to your community? How ethical will you be in the decisions and the choices that you make? How will you keep yourself informed? How will you make a difference?

Thought provoking!

Look at these young people and their questions. What answers would you give to each question?

6. Why do some people say, 'That'll never work!'?

4. Is anyone really listening to young people?

7. Who can help us to make things happen?

9. Why don't we believe the words, 'Yes We Can!'?

3. Why should my vote count?

5. Will our Action change anything?

8. How can I improve my community?

10. Why is there no 'I' in 'Team'?

11. How can I persuade others?

12. Why not make a start right now?

2. How can I influence people who make decisions?

1. I'd like to make a difference to the world, but what can one person do?

13. Does anyone really care what we think?

1. _____
2. _____
3. _____
4. _____
5. _____
6. _____
7. _____
8. _____
9. _____
10. _____
11. _____
12. _____
13. _____

ECO-UNESCO competition and award

You could take part in a competition as a CSPE action! Check out the Young Environmentalist Awards organised by ECO-UNESCO (you can find them online). Answer the questions below to find out about it.

WHO IS ECO-UNESCO?

ECO-UNESCO is Ireland's environmental education and youth organisation, affiliated to the World Federation of UNESCO clubs, centres and associations.

ECO-UNESCO'S AIMS ARE TO:

- Raise environmental awareness, understanding and knowledge of the environment among young people
- Promote the protection and conservation of the environment
- Promote the personal development of young people through practical environmental projects and activities
- Promote the ideals of UNESCO

ECO-UNESCO delivers environmental workshops, supports ECO-UNESCO Clubs, runs environmental youth events, develops education resources and delivers training.

WHAT IS THE ECO-UNESCO YOUNG ENVIRONMENTALIST AWARDS PROGRAMME?

ECO-UNESCO's Young Environmentalist Awards is an all-Ireland environmental awards programme that recognises and rewards young people who raise environmental awareness and improve the environment.

WHO SHOULD TAKE PART?

ECO-UNESCO's Young Environmentalist Awards programme is open to any group of young people in the Republic of Ireland and Northern Ireland from 10 - 18 years of age.

WHEN DO I NEED TO GET MY PROJECT IN?

ECO-UNESCO YOUNG ENVIRONMENTALIST AWARDS TIMELINE:

October-November	Free Regional Training
End of November	Project Registration Deadline
End of February	Project Submission Deadline
March & April	ECO-Den Semi-finals
May	Showcase & Awards Ceremony

Remember the sooner you register the sooner you can get support from ECO-UNESCO!

For further information, online registration, award category details, multimedia gallery, resources and more, visit: www.ecounesco.ie

1. What is the age range for taking part in the Young Environmentalist Awards?

   _____

   _____

   _____

2. Name **two** aims of ECO-UNESCO.

   (a) _____

   _____

   (b) _____

   _____

3. What is the focus of this awards programme?

   _____

   _____

4. If you are living in Northern Ireland, can you take part in this competition? Yes ☐ No ☐

5. When must you register your project?

   _____

   _____

6. When are the ECO-Den Semi-finals?

   _____

   _____

7. Create a slogan to encourage your school to get involved.

8. How are competitions of benefit to young people and schools?

   _____

   _____

   _____

Issue-tracking log

What is happening in the world today? Select an issue and track it in the media over a few days, or a few weeks. Perhaps there is a big political news story or court case from somewhere in the world? Or a humanitarian crisis you could follow? Or a story from the world of entertainment or business?

Use the template below to track the event over a period of time. Be sure to use more than one source of information. You could share information with a classmate.

The issue I am tracking is _____

Source of information	Summary of information	Comments
• • • Date Time		
Source of information	Summary of information	Comments
• • • Date Time		
Source of information	Summary of information	Comments
• • • Date Time		
Source of information	Summary of information	Comments
• • • Date Time		

Diary entry

For each day of your action, fill in your diary: what you did and when you did it. What tasks did you have to complete? What important information or skills did you learn?

Day and Date		Day and Date	
08:00		**Tasks**	
10:00			
12:00			
14:00			
16:00		**Information/skills**	
18:00			

Day and Date		Day and Date	
08:00		**Tasks**	
10:00			
12:00			
14:00			
16:00		**Information/skills**	
18:00			

Lesson reflections

The main theme/topic of this lesson

A description of what happened during the lesson

Important skills I used during this lesson

Important facts I learned in this lesson

My reflections on this lesson

Something I feel strongly about

An issue I feel strongly about/found interesting is

_____
_____
_____
_____
_____
_____
_____

I feel strongly about this issue/found this issue really interesting because

_____
_____
_____
_____
_____
_____

What I can do about this issue

_____
_____
_____
_____
_____
_____
_____

What others can do about this issue
(e.g. school, the community, the local authority, the government, the EU, the global community)

_____
_____
_____
_____
_____
_____

Research I did into the issue

_____
_____
_____
_____
_____
_____

Photo record
Photographs of key stages/events of my action

Photo 1 Title: _____

What's going on: _____

_____

_____

Photo 2 Title: _____

What's going on: _____

_____

_____

Photo 3 Title: _____

What's going on: _____

_____

_____

Committee, group or team meeting record

Date of committee meeting: _____

Names of participants: _____

_____

_____

_____

Agenda for meeting:

- Item 1: _____
- Item 2: _____
- Item 3: _____
- Item 4: _____
- Item 5: _____

Decisions from this meeting:

Actions to be taken	By whom	By what date

Thinking about teamwork

How did your committee, group or team get on?

FOLENS
Wellbeing

Questions	Yes	No
Overall, do you think that yours was a good team?		
Did everyone listen well to each other?		
Did I listen well to the other members?		
Did everyone join in with the work to be done?		
Which task was done best?		
Which task, if any, could have been done better?		
Did I play my part in the action?		
Were there many ideas and suggestions made and were they thought through properly?		
Did everyone get a fair chance to make suggestions?		
Did everyone get the chance to speak?		
Was anyone in charge?		
Did anyone get angry?		
Was anyone too bossy?		

What do you think makes a good committee, group or team?

_____
_____
_____
_____
_____
_____

When doing another action what, if anything, would you do differently? Why?

_____
_____
_____
_____
_____
_____
_____

When you have completed this reflection, discuss your answers with your team.

Action planning tool

These pages should help you to plan your action and keep you all on track.

What are you trying to achieve with your action?

_____

_____

_____

_____

_____

_____

_____

Action title

_____

_____

Who is responsible for what?

_____

_____

_____

_____

_____

_____

_____

_____

_____

_____

How are you going to do your action?

_____
_____
_____
_____
_____
_____
_____
_____
_____

What skills/expertise are you going to need?

_____
_____
_____
_____
_____
_____
_____
_____
_____

What teams, committees or groups are you going to need to set up?

_____
_____
_____
_____
_____
_____
_____
_____
_____

How will you track or record your action?

_____
_____
_____
_____
_____
_____

Research record

Doing research and gathering information is an important part of all actions. This page will help you to keep track of the sources you use.

Publications (books, journals, newspapers, magazines, brochures and leaflets)

Title of publication 1: _____

_____

_____

Author: _____

Title of publication 2: _____

_____

_____

Author: _____

Title of publication 3: _____

_____

_____

Author: _____

Internet/Online searches

Website 1 (url): _____

Found information on: _____

_____

_____

_____

Website 2 (url): _____

Found information on: _____

_____

_____

_____

Website 3 (url): _____

Found information on: _____

_____

_____

_____

Remember: Other sources may include: people, experts and organisations.

Communications plan

Make a plan to get your message across. Use the prompts below to help you.

What is your message? _____

_____

_____

_____

_____

_____

_____

Who is your audience? _____

_____

_____

_____

_____

_____

_____

_____

Who could help you with this work? _____

_____

_____

_____

_____

_____

_____

_____

How are you going to get your message across?

_____

_____

_____

_____

_____

_____

_____

Who do you need to contact? _____

_____

_____

_____

_____

_____

_____

_____

Who is on your communications team?

_____

_____

_____

_____

_____

_____

Reflection on action

FOLENS
Wellbeing

Did we achieve our action aims?

_____

_____

_____

_____

_____

_____

_____

What helped/hindered us in achieving our action aims?

_____

_____

_____

_____

_____

_____

_____

_____

_____

_____

What did you learn from doing this action?

About the issue	Skills	About yourself	About others

What would you do differently for your next action?

_____

_____

_____

_____

_____

_____

_____

_____

Action record

The title of my/our action

_____

Why we decided to do this action

1. _____

   _____

2. _____

   _____

People and organisations we worked with

People	Organisations

Teams/committees/groups we set up to do our action

Name of team	Names of team members

Why we set up these teams/groups/committees

_____

_____

_____

_____

_____

_____

_____

_____

_____

A brief description of what each group, committee or team did

A detailed step-by-step account of what my team did

A detailed step-by-step account of what my team did

Some of the skills I used while doing my/our action

One skill I used that was particularly important was

_____

_____

_____

because _____

_____

_____

_____

_____

_____

Another skill I used that was particularly important was

_____

_____

_____

because _____

_____

_____

_____

_____

_____

Other skills I have learned or developed in CSPE which will be useful in the future

_____

_____

_____

because _____

_____

_____

_____

_____

_____

Key facts that I discovered about the issue we were exploring while doing my/our action

1. _____
   _____
   _____

2. _____
   _____
   _____

3. _____
   _____
   _____

4. _____
   _____
   _____

5. _____
   _____
   _____

6. _____
   _____
   _____

7. _____
   _____
   _____

8. _____
   _____
   _____

9. _____
   _____
   _____

10. _____
    _____
    _____

My thoughts, reflections and opinions having completed my/our action

1. I think _____

_____

_____

_____

because _____

_____

_____

_____

_____

2. I feel _____

_____

_____

because _____

_____

_____

_____

_____

_____

3. I suggest/recommend _____

_____

_____

because _____

_____

_____

_____

_____

4. It is my opinion that _____

_____

because _____

_____

_____

_____

_____

_____

My four wishes for the world

Imagine you have four wishes for the world. Write your wishes in the clouds below.

A wish I have for the world is _____
_____
_____
_____

A wish I have for the world is _____
_____
_____
_____

A wish I have for the world is _____
_____
_____
_____

A wish I have for the world is _____
_____
_____
_____

Signpost for the future

The final activity in this book is a chance for you to plan ahead, and to think about the ways you will try to be an active, caring, thinking and responsible citizen, who knows that you have the power to make a difference!

FOLENS
Wellbeing

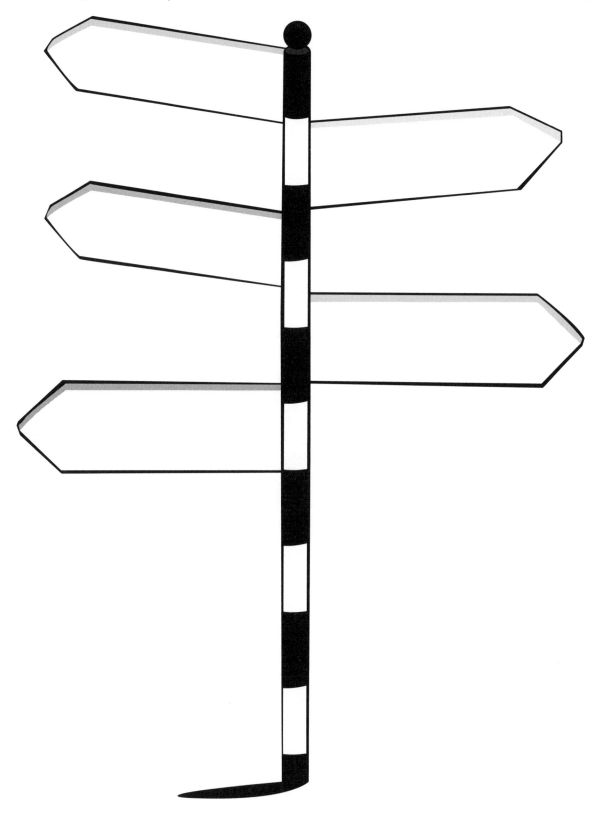

Now GO and [Make a Difference!]

TAKE CARE OF YOURSELF!

Well-Being in Post-Primary Schools

Guidelines for Mental Health Promotion and Suicide Prevention

The Well-Being Guidelines are available to download at: **www.education.ie**

Looking after your well-being is one of the most important things you can do. If you have a problem don't be shy about asking for help. Everyone has difficult times - yes, everyone!

We all need a friend or adult we trust who accepts us and believes in us. Talk to someone: maybe a family member, friend, teacher or guidance counsellor. Don't struggle alone.

Help is there for you. Ask your teachers about the **Well-Being Guidelines for Post-Primary Schools.** They give lots of advice for your school on how to work together to make things better for everyone.

SOME USEFUL WEBSITES:

Spunout.ie
Reachout.ie
Letsomeoneknow.ie

 **An Roinn Sláinte** DEPARTMENT OF HEALTH

 AN ROINN OIDEACHAIS AGUS SCILEANNA | DEPARTMENT OF EDUCATION AND SKILLS

 Feidhmeannacht na Seirbhíse Sláinte Health Service Executive

153

This Well-Being campaign is supported by the Department of Education and Skills with the co-operation of the Irish Educational Publishers Association.

Notes

Notes

Notes